DATA BASE SELECTION, DESIGN, AND ADMINISTRATION

DATA BASE SELECTION, DESIGN, AND ADMINISTRATION

By
Jon D. Clark

PRAEGER

PRAEGER SPECIAL STUDIES • PRAEGER SCIENTIFIC

Library of Congress Cataloging in Publication Data

Clark, Jon.
  Data base selection, design, and administration.

  Includes bibliographies and index.
  1. Data base management. I. Title.
QA76.9.D3C52   001.64   80-607121
ISBN 0-03-055891-3

Forms appearing in the book are taken from "A Study Guide for Accurately Defined
Systems" © copyright 1968 by NCR Corporation, Dayton, Ohio, with permission
of the copyright owner.

Published in 1980 by Praeger Publishers
CBS Educational and Professional Publishing
A Division of CBS, Inc.
521 Fifth Avenue, New York, New York 10017 U.S.A.

0123456789 **145** 987654321

Printed in the United States of America

PREFACE

Data base technology changed dramatically during the 1970s. The first half of the decade was characterized by rather significant developments in system capability; the latter half of the decade offered a general maturing of the data base concept. The management of the data resource by the data base administrator (DBA) has evolved as well. Instead of being dominated by purely technical problems, there is a mix of technical and managerial issues.

Technical problems have been well covered by the literature, including a number of excellent textbooks. The evolution toward managerial topics has not occurred; therefore, the purpose of this text is to fill this void. The general approach taken is taxonomic; all problems faced by the DBA are classified into a number of categories and the solutions to them are correspondingly classified. This book is intended to be used by the entry-level professional DBA as well as an intermediate college student of data base systems.

A number of people deserve credit for the book. In particular, thanks are due to Ginger Wilhelmi for research assistance and editorial comment; David H. Dial, friend and colleague, for laying out the general structure of the book and, in particular, Chapter 14, which concerns auditing data base systems; Dr. E. J. DeMaris, department head of Accounting and Information Systems at North Texas State University, for his continual support; and Becky Molidor and Susan Mulroy for typing the final manuscript. Any errors that remain are, of course, mine.

CONTENTS

PART V:

IMPLEMENTATION

LIST OF TABLES

LIST OF FIGURES

PART I

ESSENTIAL TERMS AND CONCEPTS

INTRODUCTION

The terminology of data base systems, like that of data processing in general, is far from standardized. In addition, many of those embarking on a career in data processing have received little, if any, formal training in the subject. It is, therefore, appropriate that an entire section of this book be devoted to developing the necessary terms and concepts of data base management systems (DBMSs).

Although in most instances popularly approved terminology will be used, in a few cases, such as in physical file design, the terminology of the "experts" will be employed. Naturally, the development of a data base language will not be the function of only this section; succeeding sections will also introduce necessary terms and concepts. The function of Part I is, then, to provide the reader with sufficient knowledge to pursue many of the particular subjects that follow.

This section is composed of four chapters, each with a special task. Chapter 1 will provide a basic working definition of data base, followed by two models: one of the operational environment in which a DBMS works, and the other a conception of a generalized DBMS. Chapter 2 will discuss, as issues, the classic advantages and, perhaps more important, the disadvantages of DBMS technology. Chapter 3's role is to present, en masse, a host of terms and concepts related to data base technology. Finally, Chapter 4 provides a taxonomy of data base system types and discusses each from a number of viewpoints.

1

OPERATIONAL ENTITIES

A DEFINITION OF DATA BASE

The number of definitions of data base present in the literature are numerous. For practical purposes what is important is not so much what they say, but, rather, what they imply regarding limitations on the users. These limitations are ultimately translated into logical and physical data processing terms. For example, a number of definitions say simply: "Data base is a stored collection of records used by application systems." The operational problem with this definition is that virtually all conventional file systems meet the requirements whereas data base is something different and more advanced.

The key might be in a popularized notion of data base, which is shown in Figure 1.1. A number of points can be derived from it:

1. There are a number and a variety of users; some in batch, others on-line.

2. The physical data base is conceived of as a total, singular unit.

3. Within the data base are stored records of importance to the individual users and, most important, the records are frequently overlapping (note records assessed by users 1, 3, and 4).

Points 1 and 3 force the modification of the initial definition, for the only way overlapping records can be provided to two or more users is

FIGURE 1.1: A Notion of a Data Base System

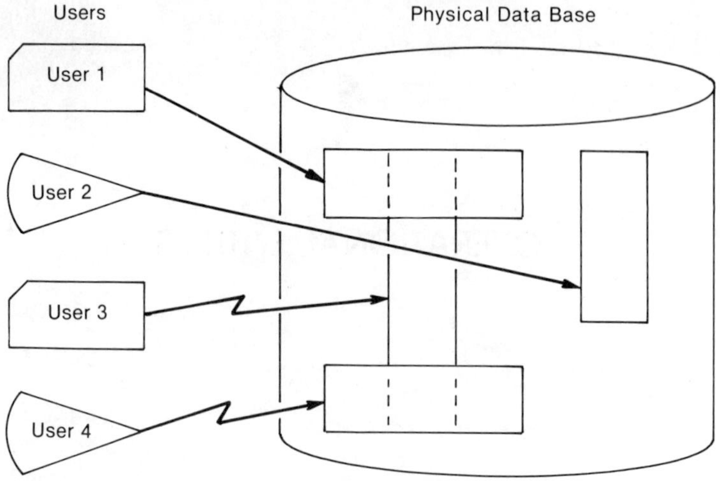

through integration. Thus, the resulting definition becomes: "Data base is a stored collection of integrated records used by two or more application systems."

Now that a working definition of data base exists, a statement regarding its purpose would be useful. Chapter 2 spends a great deal of effort discussing the issues involved in specific advantages and disadvantages of data base technology; what is needed here is simply the general goals of this technology. Briefly stated they are:

1. To handle the data requirements of a dynamic environment. Many of the advantages of data base relate to its ability to facilitate planned and organized change. This may occur in two primary areas: applications and data. Applications migrate over time because of the changing needs of the firm in general and the manager in particular. Problems change and the way in which they are solved must correspondingly be modified. Not only do the applications migrate, but, also, the data requirements tend to shift over time. This may even occur with a static-applications environment. For example, consider the possibility of the number of exceptions in a reporting application increasing throughout the years.

2. To facilitate change, control over the data resource must be enhanced. It must be enhanced over that which exists in a discrete file system; that is, a nondata-base environment. One method, that of data base, uses the principles of controlled data redundancy and centralized coordination and control over the physical resource through the DBMS and the recognized responsibility center, the data base administrator (DBA).

THE DBMS OPERATIONAL ENVIRONMENT

There are a variety of operational entities present in a typical DBMS environment. By understanding these and the relationships among them, the advantages and disadvantages of the technology will become clear. Figure 1.2 contains a model of the operational environment, the entities, and their relationships.

As can be seen in the figure there are six major entities or components to the system. Number 1, the user group, consists of all requesters of data, either on-line or in a batch mode. These requests may be of three basic types: read-data, modify-data, and add-delete-data (these will be further described in the next chapter). All requests for data are made through the DBMS.

Number 2, the DBMS, receives requests from the user group, as well as from application programmers and the DBA. To satisfy these requests, the software system must retrieve, write, or modify data on Numbers 3 and 4 (the data base and/or the data dictionary/directory [DD/D]).

Number 3, the data base, is the physical repository of all user data. It contains the physical representation of all data that a user might wish to retrieve, or, possibly, the data required to derive the user's information.

The data dictionary/directory, Number 4, contains meta-data or data about data.

The DD/D has a variety of uses. The user group may make inquiries through the DBMS to determine what information of interest is contained in the data base; the application programmers may derive the required record descriptions from it to write their application programs; and the DBA will store record descriptions that the DBA, and only the DBA, is allowed to define.

The application programmer, Number 5, must write code to process user requests. To do so, the record description of the user's data must be defined, and these definitions, though not controlled by the programmer, are available to the programmer in the DD/D.

Finally, the DBA, Number 6, controls the information resource by performing a variety of activities. Two of the most obvious of these are the generation of data descriptions and setting user access policies to be enforced by the DBMS based on information such as security codes contained in the DD/D.

Now that the operational entities and their relationships have been defined, several critical interfaces must be denoted. Each of these will receive further discussion in Section III. The user-DBA interface is much more complex than is apparent from Figure 1.1. All users must receive permission to retrieve data through the DBMS from the DBA. In addition, the DBA must perform a number of other functions including mediating con-

FIGURE 1.2: DBMS Operational Environment

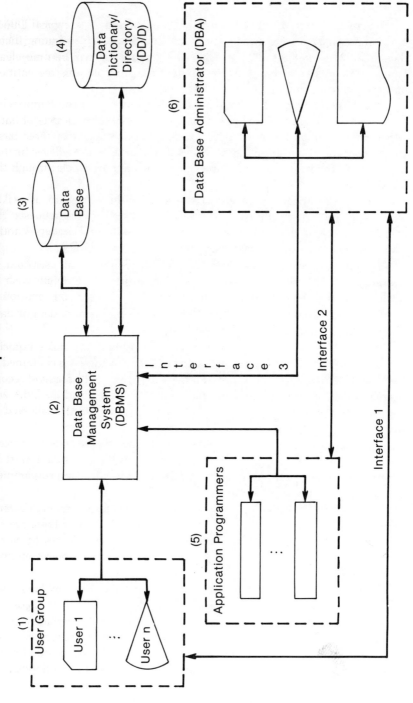

flicting user demands and training users in the methods of data base so they can exploit its advantages.

The programmer-DBA interface, though implemented partially and formally through the DBMS, also has other attributes. For example, the application programmer is never permitted to define data requirements to be ultimately stored in the DD/D without the express permission of the DBA, for to do so could potentially lead to subversion of the security provisions of the data base system. In fact, many data processing departments have the data definitions defined by the DBA, who in turn permits them to be mapped into the programs written by the applications programmers. This is a particularly important procedure since the compromising of data in an integrated system has firm-wide repercussions, rather than, for example, only function-wide.

Finally, the DBA-DBMS interface is important since it is here that management of the data resource occurs for operational efficiency. It is also here that data processing technology can be applied to data processing problems, those of the DBA. By monitoring various operational characteristics of the system, the DBA can either have the DBMS enforce standards of operation (for example, only accepting approved data definitions from the DD/D) or use the DBMS as a decision support system for the entire activity.

All of the operational entities and their corresponding relationships and interfaces form a hardware/software/human complex, the objective of which is to facilitate integrated storage, retrieval, and control of the information resource.

THE CODASYL MODEL OF OPERATION

CODASYL (The Conference on Data Systems Languages) was formed in May 1959, to consider the question of high-level languages for business, and led to the specification of COBOL as a common business-oriented language. After its reorganization in 1968, the data base task group (DBTG) was formed. The DBTG developed, among standards for DBMSs, a conceptualization of operation [1]. The DBTG model of DBMS operation is one relating to the functions performed by a number of software/data components all mapped onto the primary and secondary storage of a conventional computing system. These components, or functional units, are:

    1. Operating system: As in all conventional computing systems, this is the software system used to globally allocate system resources to individual user programs. In its role it accepts requests directly from the DBMS.

    2. Data base management system: a software system that accepts requests from user programs (may originate from users, applications

programmers, or the DBA), and, by access to the logical and physical descriptions of data contained in the schema and sub-schema, passes certain parameters to the operating system so the request may be carried out.

3. Schema: the global description of the data base, primarily consisting of physical placement information. The schema is written in the schema data definition language (DDL). The schema DDL is hardware independent, and, therefore, another language called the device/media control language (DMCL) is used to provide the global data base/hardware mapping information. The DMCL, since it is hardware dependent, is not and probably will not be standardized.

4. Sub-Schema: the user program-specific description of data, which may be quite different from that of the schema. For example, a user program may conceive of data in specific sequence while, physically, it is not stored sequentially. The sub-schema is written in the sub-schema DDL.

5. User-program: typically a superset of some host language, such as COBOL, with a number of enhancements in the form of high-level verbs for search, read, and write operations. The program is written in what CODASYL refers to as the data manipulation language (DML).

6. System buffers: a staging area into which the data base is assembled prior to being passed to the user program.

7. User working area: the area within a program's controllable address space that stores data from the data base and the system buffers.

8. System buffers: locations continually monitored by the operating system, indicating execution status of the user programs and whether they are waiting for data to be transferred.

9. Data-base: the physical repository of user data stored in secondary storage.

The operation of a generalized DBMS can best he demonstrated by tracing the actions taken by each of the functional components defined in accomplishing a request for data. Each of the numbered steps refers to an action taking place between two or more components of the system contained in Figure 1.3, and represented by numbered lines and arrows.

1. A user program places a call (request) for data to the DBMS. All calls for service of the DBMS are made in the DML.

2. The DBMS analyzes the call and supplements the arguments (parameters) provided in the call with information contained in the schema and sub-schema. Since the sub-schema describes the data as it is conceived by the user program (there is one sub-schema for each user program) and the schema describes that conceived by the whole system, one can be mapped into the other, permitting the location of the desired data.

3. On the basis of the call for services of the DBMS and the information contained in the schema and sub-schema, requests for physical input/output (I/O) operations by the operating system are executed.

4. The operating system interacts with secondary storage, in which the data base resides.

FIGURE 1.3: DBTG Conceptual Data Base Management System

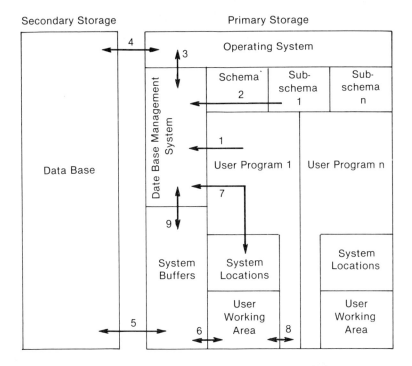

5. The operating system transfers data between secondary storage and the system buffers.

6. The DBMS transfers data as required to fulfill the call between the system buffers and the user working area. Any required data transformation between that of secondary storage and the user working area is handled by the DBMS during this step. For example, security policies may require encryption of stored data; in this step it can be deciphered, then encrypted prior to being written to the data base.

7. The DBMS provides status information to the user program that has issued the call (for example, currency status and error status).

8. The data in a user program's user working area may be manipulated as required, using the facilities of the DML. Note, however, that the contents of the schema and sub-schema may restrict certain user programs to specific types of access (for example, read only).

9. The DBMS administers the system buffers. Since these buffers are shared by all user programs serviced by the DBMS, the user programs must have their activities controlled by the DBMS, so, for example, the classic problem of concurrent update with resulting loss of information does not occur.

SUMMARY OF CHAPTER CONTENTS

The purpose of this chapter was to present two operational models of a generalized data base system. The first model consisted of entities both internal and external to the computer system, including user, application programmer, DBA, DBMS, DD/D, and the physical data base, and how each of these was related functionally. The second model was CODASYL's conceptual hardware/software system, which provided a graphic demonstration of activities performed to accomplish a user's request for data.

Before proceeding to Chapter 2, in which issues of advantages and disadvantages are discussed, consider the complexity of the technology just presented, for it is this complexity that must be exploited to its fullest to make DBMS technology cost-effective.

REFERENCE

1. CODASYL, *Data Base Task Group Report* (New York: Association for Computing Machinery, 1971).

2

POTENTIAL EFFECTS OF DATA BASE
MANAGEMENT SYSTEMS

INTRODUCTION

Authors, vendors, and practitioners have made a variety of claims regarding DBMS technology in general. In particular, however, these may or may not apply. The purpose of this chapter is to present many of these claims as issues, thereby giving the reader sufficient background to make a judgment in most particular cases. The taxonomy of DBMS impacts presented in the next section will be used as a vehicle to this end.

A TAXONOMY OF DBMS EFFECTS

Although all commercial DBMSs claim additional capabilities over their traditional file-processing counterparts, these must be paid for in some fashion. The taxonomy contained in the following outline table reflects this tradeoff by categorizing all impacts into either advantages or disadvantages. In addition, the advantages are broken into user-directed (indicating that there is a user-logical benefit) and operational (suggesting a data processing benefit). The disadvantages primarily relate to direct financial costs and several inherent problems associated with changing user thinking and the required management support to insure the success of the system.

TABLE 2.1: A Taxonomy of DBMS Impacts

Advantages
  User-Directed
    1. Complexity of Relationships
    2. Centralized Control of Data
       security
       integrity
    3. Ease of Search
  Operational
    1. Controlled Redundancy
    2. Independance
       data
       device
    3. Accessibility
       real-time
       parallel
    4. Ease of Creating, Restructuring, Updating, and Maintaining
    5. Flexibility
Disadvantages
  Costs
    1. Initial
       cost of DBMS
       installation
    2. Continuing
  Complexity
  User Indoctrination
  Likelihood of Success

The Advantages

User-Directed

User-directed advantages are those that are of direct benefit to the user, typically in terms of logical capability, and were not available, at least to the same extent, in a non-DBMS environment. That these capabilities exist does not imply that they will be present in any specific system.

Complexity of Relationships.   The primary constraint on data structure complexity in a traditional file system is one of accommodating large numbers of files and the number of accesses it would take to assemble data from them. Figure 2.1 pictorially describes the problem.

To assemble the required data for a complex request to a file system, many individual files must be maintained on-line, each of which must be accessed. It would not be difficult to make a request calling for more storage

FIGURE 2.1: Comparison of Relationships Supported

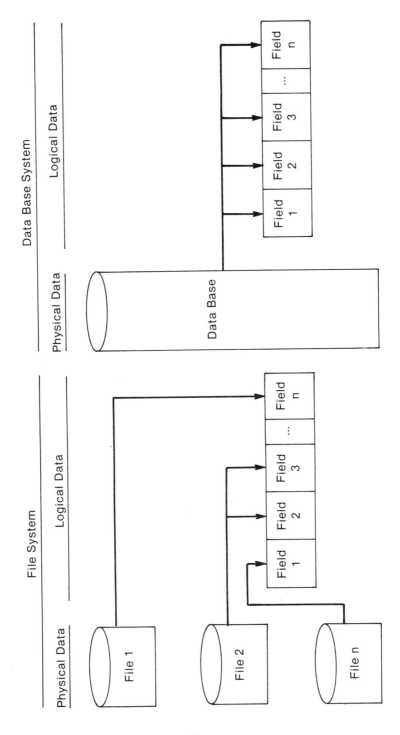

devices than are available on a typical machine. In a DBMS environment, however, the individual files are integrated, thus reducing most redundancy. Although the data base is much larger than the individual files of the file system, it nevertheless is all available on-line. In addition, the number of accesses to the data base is likely to be less than if individual files were used. The result is that much more complex relationships can effectively be handled by using the data base approach.

Centralized Control of Data.   All calls for data made by application programs must be channeled into the DBMS because it is here that the mapping from logical to physical records is made. Once the mapping occurs, the appropriate parameters are passed to the operating system, which carries out the access procedure. In a file-processing system, however, all requests for data go immediately to the operating system. Though both of these methods may appear to be centralized to some extent, only the DBMS attempts to control access down to the element level and may even regulate the types of instructions performed on each element.

Centralized control of data enhances security, privacy, and integrity protection. Security refers to the protection of data against accidental or intentional disclosure, modifications, or destruction. Privacy is concerned with the right of the individual or an organization to determine when, how, and to what extent information about them is to be transmitted to others. Therefore, security is necessary but not sufficient for privacy. Both are enhanced in a DBMS because of centralization of control since all calls to the data base must be given access permission prior to being given the necessary information to process the call. Also, since redundancy is limited to a great extent in a DBMS environment, other opportunities to gather or subvert the same information are reduced. Data integrity exists when the data element values do not differ from their source documents and, therefore, have not been accidentally or maliciously altered, disclosed, or destroyed. Integrity, too, is enhanced because of the relatively strict access policies that may be imposed and the limited redundancy that tends to reduce many potential transaction errors.

Ease of Search.   Users of a DBMS, with very little knowledge of its structure, may make requests for data. This is because all calls to the data base made at the application or user level simply involve the logical description of the data elements required. The DBMS then resolves the problem of physical location by methods that do not affect the user.

There has been a dramatic trend toward advanced language design used in conjunction with data base technology. Virtually every DBMS vendor markets a query language that lends itself to the casual user.* Not

*The conception of supporting casual users who have little, if any, vested interest in computer operations was applied to data base by Codd [(2), (3)].

only are the query languages interactive but also highly nonprocedural. Boolean operators are typically used to facilitate the ease with which complex search strategies may be made. For example, a system called LADDER [1] is capable of taking a query such as "What is the length of the Kennedy?" (the Kennedy being a ship), and translating it into the query

((NAM EQ JOHN#F. KENNEDY) (? LENGTH)),

where LENGTH is the name of the length field, NAM the name of the ship name field, and JOHN#F.KENNEDY the value of the NAM field for the record concerned with the Kennedy. The response is simply

(LENGTH 1072 feet).

More complex actions may be specified as well. Using CASDAL [4] one may request concerning the employee SMITH, get his department and salary, transfer him to the TOY department, and increase his salary by $500, and then verify the result by retrieving his record after modification.

```
IF EMP.NAME='SMITH' THEN DO:
OUTPUT(EMP.SAL,EMP.DEPT).
UPDATE(EMP.DEPT='TOY',EMP.SAL=*+500),
OUTPUT(EMP)
END;
```

Although this requires some knowledge of basic data processing procedures, such as output and update, it nevertheless is quite easy for a casual user to employ for complex manipulations.

Operational Advantages

Not all benefits of a DBMS accrue to its users; some very important ones are derived operationally by data processing. The following sections discuss many of these advantages.

Controlled Redundancy.   One of the major operational advantages of DBMS technology is data control—control that is possible only through the limitation of the number of physical occurrences of any data element. In traditional file systems, control is lost in many cases because of the extreme number of occurrences of an item in storage and the corresponding difficulty in recording where each exists and maintaining each as changes occur.

Very frequently it has been stated that zero redundancy is both practical and desirable; this does not recognize the large amount of overhead inherent in current-generation DBMSs and the practical necessity to fine tune them in various ways to achieve acceptable performance. Redundancy may be designed selectively into a storage system so performance is enhanced. An example of this might be an on-line query system with which multiple users require simultaneous access to certain data elements. Redundancy allows parallel access; hence, improved user response time.

Commercial systems are beginning to recognize the advantage of planned redundancy and are redesigning their systems to handle it. Unfortunately, it is left to the DBA to decide on an ad hoc basis where redundancy is appropriate.

Independence.   One purpose of a DBMS is to make user requests for data, their logical implementation, and the physical arrangement of the data as independent of one another as possible. This allows the physical data base to be changed without affecting user requests, perhaps for reasons of efficiency, and allows users to change their requests without necessitating a change in the physical data base organization, as might be required in a traditional file environment.

Commercial systems vary in the degree of opaqueness they provide between the user and the supporting storage structure. In general, this opaqueness can be of three types: logical data independence, physical data independence, and physical device independence.

Logical data independence is provided, to a degree, in most commercial systems by having the DBMS dynamically map logical requests into the storage structure. The schema and sub-schema are used, in part, for this purpose. Although data names are the only requirement in the call statements of many DMLs, the user must be aware of the logical arrangement of the data or the request for data cannot be processed. Hence, all commerical systems are access-path dependent; only those logical access paths implemented in the system may be used in any request for data.

Physical data independence relates to the degree to which logical and physical data are tied. For example, in both FORTRAN and COBOL the description of the physical characteristics of data to be accessed is imbedded within the program; therefore, any change to the data values must be matched by a corresponding change in the application programs or user requests; thus, there is no physical data independence. In commercial systems, however, some changes can be made to the physical representation of data without affecting all of the user requests requiring the item. Although field sizes must be consistent, data coding, or encryption, can be done, or changed, with no effect on the individual requests.

Device independence is a desirable characteristic of any computerized information processing system (IPS) because of application and data migration. As access patterns and the technology of computer systems change, it becomes desirable to change the physical placement of data, perhaps even the device types (tape to disk or vice versa). If device independence exists, it can be done with no changes required to user requests. Practically speaking, this is difficult to achieve; nevertheless, a degree of device independence is provided in most systems. The amount of independence is typically limited to devices with different storage capacities and access speeds within a class of systems (such as disk or drum). No commercial systems allow sufficient freedom to swith device types without an effect on the application programs.

Accessibility.   DBMSs enhance the capability of parallel access of data and real-time query and update. Parallel access of data by two or more applications is extremely important in a data base environment since the data is physically integrated and, hence, there are no dedicated files servicing each process requiring data. Parallel access of data is also difficult to achieve, because two or more applications may attempt to update the same data item concurrently. One of two methods may be used in this case: lock out all processes after the first until the update has been made, or allow both (or any number of) processes to update their own copy of the original item's value and then reconcile all of the updates done in parallel. If updating is not required, parallel access is not a practical problem. Although many commercial systems offer only the first method, the second is beginning to grow in popularity.

Although real-time systems were in existence long before data base technology developed, their use has grown, in part, because of increasing data base applications. There are two reasons for this: users may work with more complex data relationships, and the data is physically stored in an integrated form that is easily stored on-line. It is therefore reasonable that data base technology has facilitated on-line accessibility.

Ease of Creation, Restructure, Update, and Maintenance.   As with all data management facilities used in a traditional file system environment, DBMSs offer utilities that create, restructure, update, and maintain the data base. A surprising aspect of these utilities is that they are not much more sophisticated than previous-generation data management aids. In fact, no vendor (except IBM [5], with its Data Base Design Aid) offers any tool for determining into what form the data base is to be created or restructured. This is a particularly weak area that is of critical importance since the economic success of the supported systems depends, in part, on the initial file design.

Software to assist in monitoring data base performance is becoming available. Although this software does not explicitly prescribe design changes, it does indicate where high activity exists and, thus, where effort for efficient design should be expended.

Flexibility.   Although design flexibility is an attribute of data base systems from a user's point of view, operational flexibility is also important when computer efficiency is of value. Much of the flexibility provided by a DBMS is from the delay in binding. All logical references to data must be resolved to the physical level. This may occur during coding of the program or as late as program execution. In other than a DBMS environment it typically occurs at compilation time, when all of the physical attributes of the data to be accessed are considered in setting up the access routines. The advantage of binding at code-generation time is that it need only be done once, regardless of the number of executions of that program; that is, it is very efficient. If done at execution time, however, it must be done prior to each call for data and is therefore costly. Most important, however, it is very flexible since large arrays (or whatever other mechanism might be used) do not need to be set up to handle the largest situations possible.

Disadvantages

A price must be paid for all of the advantages offered by data base technology, and often it is in terms of a direct financial charge. Both the financial and nonfinancial costs attributed to a DBMS installation will be examined next.

Financial Costs

The financial costs are of two types: initial expenditures or start-up costs, and continuing or operational charges; each will be examined in the following sections.

Initial Costs.   Data base setup costs include the cost of the DBMS package and any programmer/analyst efforts required during conversion from the existing system. Table 2.1 contains several financial and nonfinancial costs. In most cases DBMS package costs range from $10,000 to $140,000. Depending on the vendor this may or may not include such extras as data dictionary/directory or on-line data query software.

The initial cost of the DBMS may be relatively insignificant when compared to the installation costs, however. Although typically not paid to the DBMS vendor, it is, nevertheless, paid in terms of programmer/analyst time involved in the following setup activities:

1. Data dictionary/directory definition, including resolution of data synonyms and homonyms. This typically requires the analysis of hundreds of data elements by all user departments and, therefore, should not be underestimated in terms of time expenditure.

TABLE 2.2: Some Financial and Non-Financial Costs of DBMSs

Product	Vendor	Minimum Storage Rqd.	Basic System Cost-Max Cost
ADABAS	Software AG of North America	200K bytes	$66-132,000
DATA COM/DB	Insyte Datacom	32K bytes	$34-40,000
DBS-10	Digital Equipment	32K 36-bit words	$27,500
DBMS-20	Digital Equipment	64 512-word pages	$27,500
DL/1 DOS/VS	IBM	98K bytes	$395 per month
DM-IV/I-D-S-II	Honeywell	12K words	$893 per month
DMS-II	Burroughs	180K bytes	to $24,000 (lower for smaller versions)
DMS/90	Sperry Univac	131K byte words	No charge to Univac customers
DMS-1100	Sperry Univac	15K words	No charge to Univac customers
IDMS	Cullinane	55K bytes	$50,000
IMS	IBM	128K bytes	$646-950 per month
INQUIRE	Infodata Systems	40K bytes	$70-140,000
Model 204	Computer Corporation of America	280K bytes	$70-130,000
System 2000	MRI Systems	140K bytes	$30,000
TOTAL	Cincom Systems	8K bytes	$10-45,000

19

2. Data base planning for applications to be continued in the new environment and development of proposed applications, as well as a schedule for implementation.

3. Data base design involving the analysis of required logical relationships and the corresponding physical placement of data. Additional hardware may have to be acquired to accommodate the physical data base.

4. User, programmer, and analyst education in data base concepts so the advantages may be fully exploited and costs minimized.

5. Conversion of data and existing application programs, development and implementation of new systems, and the documentation of all systems.

Point 4 cannot be overemphasized. If traditional file processing techniques are allowed to continue, operational costs of the DBMS will become inflated, the advantages that otherwise might have been exploited will not offset the costs, and the likelihood of failure of the conversion will be increased.

Continuing Costs.   Continuing or operational costs consist of three types: access, hardware, and personnel. Access costs typically are higher in a data base environment because of the delay in binding (see Chapter 3). The delay in binding logical items to physical locations requires that this mapping occur during each access for every data item, rather than, for example, once during compilation of the application program. In addition, the more complex logical structures (see Chapter 3) require correspondingly more complex access paths; hence, more overhead.

Additional hardware may also be necessitated by a DBMS for two reasons: the DBMS occupies between 8K and 256K bytes of primary storage, with options for more; and more memory, both primary and secondary, is often added to compensate in part for the otherwise poor execution times of application programs that result from added overhead. Rarely is the practical requirement of additional storage indicated in the descriptive literature of the DBMS.

The inherent complexity of a DBMS and the associated technical problems that frequently occur require a high level of systems programming expertness. In fact, the DBA is frequently a person with systems programming experience. The application programmers may have to be upgraded when changing from a traditional file system to a data base. Although it may not be obvious at first why this is necessary, it has occurred frequently in the field. For example, writing file descriptions prior to deciding on appropriate access paths, as might be done in a file system environment, is likely to lead to very inefficient data base operation, because of calling and transferring attribute values that are not required. In addition, the accessing of attributes that are not required for that application program may cause the lockout of other programs that legitimately need them.*

---

*See Clark and Hoffer [6] for a complete description of these operational problems.

Complexity

Although the effect of DBMS software complexity can be felt in terms of direct costs, it can also affect a variety of data processing operations:

1. Technical problems faced by the DBA will dominate those of a managerial nature.
2. Quick, simple fixes of software may not be possible.
3. Difficulty of making changes may discourage fine tuning and, hence, more inefficient operations.
4. Maintenance of the DBMS will consume large amounts of system and personnel resources.
5. Resident personnel may have difficulty diagnosing particular problems.

The extreme complexity of most DBMSs contributes, of course, to their high initial cost, and the use of system resources (in particular, primary memory), all of which were discussed in previous sections.

User Indoctrination

In an informal study, performed by the author, involving randomly selected DBAs, it was found that user indoctrination in data base concepts was important. Apparently, users have become accustomed to certain data processing concepts that are no longer relevant once a data base is implemented. One of the most serious is the concept of "own data"—the ownership of data and the physical existence of it on a discrete user-identifiable storage medium such as tape. Two things happen to invalidate this concept when a data base is implemented: the user's data is no longer in a dedicated or discrete file (in fact, it is likely to have been merged logically with many other pieces of data), and the notion that a particular user owns the data that is used is ludicrous. Consider any shared data base environment when the user and collector of certain data decides that continued collection of it is not necessary, and they subsequently do not collect it. All other users of that data, perhaps in other functional areas, who are not in a position to collect it are dependent upon the original provider. Hence, in a data base environment, responsibility must be assigned for every element and it cannot always be based on use but, instead, on efficient provision or priority for collection.

Likelihood of Success

Support by top management is crucial to the success of any DBMS. In particular, during initial design of both logical and physical structures, when large amounts of resources are being expended, top management support is necessary so shortcuts are not taken that will have subsequent and potentially disastrous effects. The problem is that the initial design effort does not have an immediate payback; therefore, it is all too attractive as a candidate for cost savings. Morgan and Soden [7] have delineated a variety of causes for failures involving information systems; these include operational, economic, technical, development, and priority failures. A common thread through these various types of failures is the taking of shortcuts that often have little short-run effect but develop into data processing disasters.

SUMMARY OF CHAPTER CONTENTS

This chapter began by developing a taxonomy of DBMS effects on users and data processing (DP) in general. These were divided into two broad categories: advantages (consisting of user-directed and operational sub-categories), and disadvantages (costs, complexity, user indoctrination, and the likelihood of success).

REFERENCES

1. G. G. Hendrix, E. D. Sacerdoti, D. Sagalowicz and J. Slocum, "Developing a Natural Language Interface to Complex Data," *ACM Transactions on Data Base Systems* 3 (June 1978) 2: 105–47.

2. E. F. Codd, "A Relational Model of Data for Large Shared Data Banks," *Communications of the ACM* 13 (June 1970) 6: 377–87.

3. E. F. Codd, "Further Normalization of the Data Base Relational Model," *Data Base Systems: Courant Computer Sciences Symposia Series* 6, Englewood Cliffs, N.J.: Prentice-Hall, 1971, pp. 65–98.

4. S. Y. W. Su and A. Emam, "CASDAL: CASSM's DATA Language," *ACM Transactions on Data Base Systems* 3 (March 1978) 1: 57–91.

5. N. Raver and G. H. Hubbard, "Automated Logical Data Base Design: Concepts and Applications," *IBM Systems Journal* (1977) 3: 287–312.

6. J. D. Clark and J. A. Hoffer, "A Procedure for the Determination of Attribute Access Probabilities," *Proceedings of ACM-SIGMOD,* Austin, Texas (1978): 110–17.

7. H. L. Morgan and J. V. Soden, "Understanding MIS Failures," *Data Base* 5 (Winter 1973) 2, 3, 4: 157–71.

4

A TAXONOMY OF SYSTEM TYPES

INTRODUCTION

The purpose of this chapter is to present a series of three taxonomies of DBMSs so the full range of commercial and theoretical alternatives are known for purposes of selection. It is extremely important that the class of DBMS match closely the user's requirements. The taxonomies to be discussed relate to standardized versus specialized systems; procedural versus nonprocedural data manipulation languages (DMLs); and linear, tree, network, and relational data models. Finally, having presented the theoretical types of DBMSs, a general feature analysis will be offered that addresses not only the factors of the various typologies, but also a number of others that may be of practical interest such as cost, and memory requirements.

STANDARDIZED VERSUS SPECIALIZED SYSTEMS

The issue of standardized versus specialized DBMSs was an important one seven years ago [(1, 2)]; it is no less so today. Data processing has relatively few standards, except in the area of programming languages (for example, COBOL and FORTRAN), as is appropriate and practical for a rapidly advancing technology. DBMS technology is even younger and more dynamic, and yet the issue just cited is both timely and important, as will be seen from the itemized subissues involved. This section will take a two-layered approach to the discussion of the issues: in general, the tradeoff between a standardized versus nonstandardized (or specialized) DBMS, and the problems associated with the CODASYL Data Base Task Group (DBTG) recommendation (the only existing standard of any practical consequence).

The following outline contains the major subissues. The standardized approach generally offers four major advantages. Transferability from hardware vendor to hardware vendor as well as from DBMS to DBMS

Why a Common Approach

Transferability:
  • applications from computer to computer
  • applications from DBMS to DBMS to exploit costs or efficiency
Personnel: easier to find trained personnel
Users: need only learn one set of concepts
Cost: since application interface is standardized, redevelopment of these is
    not necessary

Why a Specialized Approach

Efficiency:
  • application programming aids
  • user interfaces for efficiency and effectiveness
  • specific computer/software interface considered during DBMS
    design
Cost: only necessary to obtain DBMS with required capabilities, not full set
    as in standard
Common demand for capabilities not well established in the marketplace

would be greatly enhanced, although it is unreasonable to assume the existence of complete transferability any more than it currently exists for COBOL, for example. Nevertheless, if would prove to be an advantage in any environment where upgrades in both hardware and software are a likely occurrence. The high cost of applications development and implementation is even higher when one is effectively committed to a specific vendor's hardware/software systems, or, worse yet, to a specific model or version of each. Personnel, particularly programmers, are also much easier to find for generalized systems. Consider the difference in the level of difficulty of finding an Autocoder versus finding a COBOL programmer. Users, although not suffering from the same replacement problems as programmers, nevertheless may find significant advantages in a standardized approach to conceptualizing systems. The difficulty and cost involved in training users to articulate their problems and system requirements should not be taken lightly; and the differences between types of DBMSs can be staggering. Regardless of what standard is used, a standard enhances a user's vested interest in developing an expertness in addition to facilitating better, and perhaps more stable, problem definitions.

The initial cost of a DBMS package may also be affected by the existence of a standard. Obviously, specialized systems may either be very expensive because of high sophistication and, therefore, development costs, or inexpensive because of the lack of many commonly required capabilities. A standardized system, although offering complete capability (in some sense), may offer it at a lower cost because there is no development cost for the standardized interfaces (DDL and DML).

The advantages of specialized systems can be quite compelling. Efficiency problems have traditionally been associated with complex systems and, therefore, data base systems are likely to have problems of this type as well. Specialized DBMSs can offer efficiency advantages over their standardized relatives in three respects: for the application programmer who may have access to special verbs or procedures in the DML for particular tasks; for the user who may have tailor-made interfaces to make data base use easy, or even feasible; and for the computer that may operate much more efficiently because of the DBMS being tailor-written for a specific machine and operating system.

Although at first it may appear contradictory, costs may also be to the advantage of specialized systems. This may be true particularly if the full set of standard features are of little value; then they need not be acquired, and other features sought instead. Related to this latter point, and a very important issue, is whether a standard set of capabilities has been recognized in the marketplace. What may be, without a doubt, a required feature for one class of user may not be for another.

Any discussion of the relative merits of standardized DBMS technology need not be done abstractly, since one already exists—that of the CODASYL DBTG [3]. The DBTG standard applies to the DDL and DML and provides a network data model based on the concept of sets. Rather than attempt to justify the various provisions of the standard, which, no doubt, are well thought out, only criticisms of it will be presented here. Note, however, that many weak points are actually weaknesses in the general state of the technical development of DBMSs and, therefore, apply to particular cases as well. According to *EDP Analyzer* [2], some of these weaknesses are:

    1. The application programmer must know the existing data structure to map record and set occurrences into areas.

2. The implementor of a system must assign data base keys and may make poor choices regarding efficiency.

3. The application programmer must know and specify within the application programs the specific access method to retrieve records or sets.

4. The application programmer must consider the side effects of various DML commands on the currency status indicators (a particular provision of the DBTG standard) and must, in some cases, suppress the updating of these indicators.

5. Concurrent update is still a problem; interface may be overlooked.

6. Sets and repeating groups are two logical structures for the same purpose; for simplicity, one should be eliminated.

7. There are a number of dependencies between the DDL and the DML such that when one is changed the other may have to be modified as well.

8. The DBA cannot always reorganize the data base without affecting application programs. This is particularly true where area contents change.

Although the issues of the standardized versus specialized DBMS controversy may in part be clear, the conclusions are not. The best thing that can happen from a consumer point of view is what actually is occurring in the marketplace; the offering by a number of firms of a standardized package as well as a wide range of specialized systems.

A TAXONOMY OF DML TYPES

Any taxonomy of DML types must include a range of alternatives from procedural to nonprocedural. Essentially, the procedural end of the spectrum is that which requires programming in the traditional sense, whereas the nonprocedural end only requires a statement of the problem but does not recommend a procedure for solution. A more useful description of this range of procedurality recognizes only three points: one on either extreme and one in the middle, as shown in Figure 4.1.

FIGURE 4.1: Procedurality Range of Data Manipulation Languages

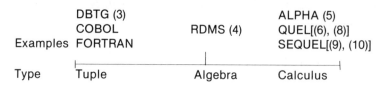

	DBTG (3)		ALPHA (5)
	COBOL	RDMS (4)	QUEL[(6), (8)]
Examples	FORTRAN		SEQUEL[(9), (10)]
Type	Tuple	Algebra	Calculus

The marked points of Figure 4.1 are defined as follows:

1. Tuple—This suggests that a programmer must define all procedures for the accessing and processing of data at the record and/or element levels, as is the case with COBOL and FORTRAN. A language of this type forces the programmer to have knowledge of many storage and access characteristics of the specific data processing environment.

2. Algebra—A language of this type requires accessor-defined procedures, but these are defined using high-level verbs such as those used in set theory: join, intersection, union, and others. The effect of this is to greatly relieve the programmer from the burdens of system-dependent specifications.

3. Calculus—The highest level of abstraction allows the programmer (in fact, the user) to simply state the problem without reference to a specific solution. The system must analyze the problem statement for consistency and completeness, then determine a solution.

The code required for these three levels of abstraction will give a more graphic demonstration of the differences in problem/solution definition complexity. The problem at hand is to find the part numbers involved in project number 15 from the following file (Table 4.1).

TABLE 4.1: Part Number/Requirements File

Part Number	Project Number	Quantity Committed
205	11	7
205	15	10
209	10	2
209	15	3
209	25	1
210	11	4
218	25	2

Table 4.2 contains the code required to accomplish this task for a tuple at a time in DBTG form, algebraic form in RDMS and, in the form of a calculus, SEQUEL.* In general, note how short and concise the algebraic and calculus forms are, but without many of the familiar, procedural details common to general-purpose programming languages. The tuple-at-a-time implementation of the DBTG contains descriptions of all procedural details: MOVEing the value of the project number for which a matching operation must be made to a reserved area; FINDing the first record of the appropriate set (file); checking to confirm whether the set specified contains any records and, if not, what action to take; a loop paragraph that repetitively FINDs records

---

*See Kim [11] for an excellent tutorial on this subject.

TABLE 4.2: Comparison of Query Languages

TUPLE (DBTG)	Algebra (RDMS)	Calculus (SEQUEL)
MOVE '15' TO INO IN J	project-involvement = PROJECT (part-number)	SELECT PART-NUMBER FROM J-P
FIND J RECORD	WHERE project-number = 15	WHERE PROJECT-NUMBER = 15
IF J-P SET EMPTY GO TO NONE-SUPPLIED		
NXT. FIND NEXT P RECORD OF J-P SET.		
IF ERROR-STATUS = 0307 GO TO ALL-FOUND		
GET P		
GO TO NXT.		

The Answer Part Number

205
209

and looks for the end of a file, at which time another action or procedure is invoked.

The algebraic implementation written in RDMS is also procedural to the extent that an operator (or operators, for more complex problems) has been specified to take a specific action out of a set of possible actions (union, intersection, difference, projection, selection, and join). In this case a projection on part number is being requested, based on the selection requirement that project number equals 15. Note that the details of finding the beginning and servicing the end of the set or file are left up to the system.

Finally, the calculus implementation written in SEQUEL, although driven by high-level operators, is nonprocedural; only the data to be retrieved, the set from which it is to be taken, and the selection criterion are specified. The algebraic operators of join, intersection, and the rest need never be used even in more complex problem formulations.

A word of caution is necessary. It is too easy to develop the notion that nonprocedural languages (calculus based) are to be preferred. This is true only under those circumstances where the user is in a poor position to choose the best means of access or where the choice is made not to exercise judgment in this regard. In all other task situations, for reasons of efficiency, it is often preferable to explicitly state the desired access path to be used.

A TAXONOMY OF DDL MODELS

Chapter 3 introduced a number of terms and concepts, some of which relate to data models. The purpose of this section is to discuss characteristics of each data model so an objective selection can be made; typically this involves operational characteristics and limitations. The four models to be discussed are: linear lists, trees, networks, and the relational model. Although, in general, these may be converted one for the other, there may be some undesirable operational effects by doing so.

To develop a sense for the capabilities and limitations of the four data models, a standard application will be defined, then implemented and discussed for each. A common application for manufacturing firms is bill-of-material processing. Typically the data base for this application system consists of sets of records for finished assemblies, subassemblies, component parts, purchased parts, and raw materials, each of which contains a code uniquely identifying a specific record among that set. Each record type contains attributes describing that type of entity, as is shown in Table 4.3. In general, applications accessing this data base attempt to draw relationships among the various records within a set and between the sets. For example, a within-the-set requirement may be to generate a listing of all purchased parts; a between-the-sets application might specify that all purchased parts and materials be listed for finished assemblies 7702 through 7708. Let us now consider the four possible data models in action.

TABLE 4.3: Example of Bill-of-Material Record Contents

Record Type/Name	Attribute Contents
1/Finished assembly	Assembly number Description Manufacturing sequence code Material Quantity
2/Subassembly	Subassembly number Description Manufacturing sequence code Material Quantity
3/Component part	Component part number Description Manufacturing sequence code Material Quantity
4/Purchased part	Purchased part number Description
5/Raw material	Raw material number Description

The first data model, linear list, can be constructed in a number of ways, but this discussion arbitrarily considers only one. As may be recalled from Chapter 3, only one entry point and one exit point is allowed to or from the list. Figure 4.2 contains a portion of a hypothetical list for the bill-of-material data base. To process the first request, involving a list of all purchased parts, the entire list must be scanned and just those records are selected that are members of the purchased part set. Since these records are likely to be uniquely identified as such, this is not difficult, although it does require a time-consuming operation. A more difficult problem is that of removing duplicate entries. Since any given purchased part may be used in a number of subassemblies, it is likely to be represented in one or more places in the list. These duplicate entries must not be printed for the requester; hence, the set of all purchased parts obtained from the list could be sorted and then a line item for each unique, purchased part number would be printed for the requester.

For the second request the list is scanned until the finished assembly record with the assembly part number 7702 is found, then those purchased parts following it, but prior to the next finished assembly, must be printed. It is also possible for duplicates to exist. These, too, must be removed (sorting is but one alternative).

A tree structure is frequently associated with bill-of-material processing and, therefore, handles in a much more natural manner the requests that have been suggested.

The logical implication of the more compact structure of the tree data model contained in Figure 4.3 is that fewer record-to-record traversals need be made to reach any desired logical record. Let us consider the two hypothesized requests for data, the first being to generate a list of all raw materials used for finished assemblies contained in the data base. This involves checking the contents of all branches of the tree; thus, full enumeration of the node contents since raw materials may be required at any level of the tree. However, if one were to be looking for a specific raw material, full enumeration could be avoided through the use of a technique called low-level coding, in which the lowest (farthest down) level at which a given material is used is known prior to the search operation. This technique cannot be used in the list model.

The second request, which requires that a list of all raw materials for finished assembly 7702 be generated, can be accomplished quite easily with the tree model since the finished assembly is found logically and immediately, although physically the computer may use a number of alternative search strategies, including direct access or serial search. Once the finished assembly is found, it can be directly associated with subordinate levels of logical records, skipping those without relevance. Low-level coding will not work in this request, because the raw material requirements of a given finished assembly are not known until all levels of the tree have been named.

**FIGURE 4.2: Bill-of-Material Application Using a
Linear List Data Model**

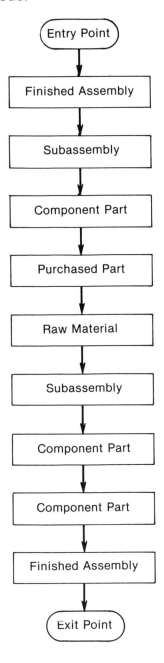

FIGURE 4.3: Bill-of-Material Application Using a Tree Data Model

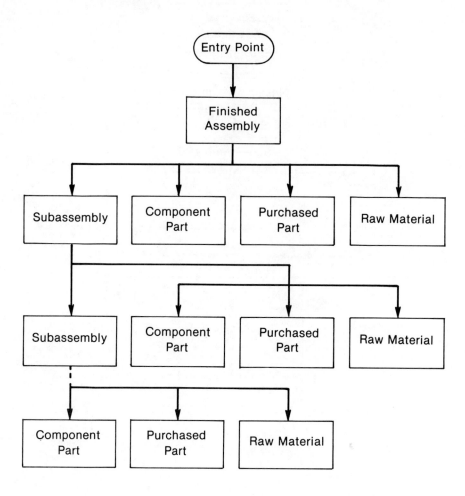

The logical advantage of the tree model over that of the list is that many irrelevant logical records need not be traversed during request processing. In addition, trees naturally handle a greater variety of the commonly found logical structures in data processing.

The network data model contained in Figure 4.4 relaxes the single-entry restriction to each node or logical record and, therefore, allows very

FIGURE 4.4: Bill-of-Material Application Using Network Data Model

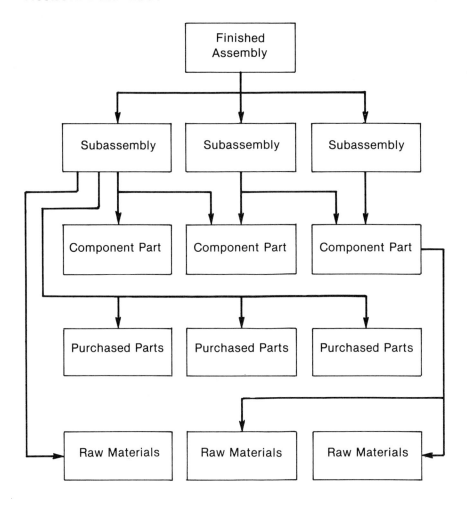

complex relationships to be represented without any logical redundancy. The fact that any single logical record can be associated with any other number of logical records makes the processing of the two hypothesized requests quite easy.

Consider request one, where a listing of all raw materials used in the data base is required. This is a trivial exercise since each raw material record exists only once; hence, filtering out the duplicates is not necessary, as it would be with the list and tree models. For request two, where a listing of all raw materials used in finished assembly 7702 is needed, the processing is easier because of this same characteristic of no logical redundancy. The network model, of the three discussed so far, is the most general; it can be used to represent any set of relationships, without the inclusion of unwanted redundancy.

There have been a number of debates regarding the relative desirability of the network and relational approaches to data models [12, 13, 14]. Although the issue, regarding which is most appropriate under any given set of circumstances, is quite complex, the essence is simply navigational. That is to say, with the network approach a user must have detailed knowledge of the data structure so the logical associations that link logical records can be navigated for retrieval or processing purposes. The relational approach does not contain linkages (sometimes referred to as representative clutter), as such, and can be used more readily by an untrained or casual user. The inherent simplicity of the relational model will become evident when the two hypothesized requests are considered. Figure 4.5 contains a representation of the relational approach to bill-of-material processing.

To derive the information required for request one (the raw material used for all finished assemblies in the data base), the contents of the Raw Material Relation need only be printed, and only those domains (attributes) of interest to the user have to be output. Very likely, however, a user will want the output in a specific sequence; this requires a sort on that domain prior to output but is a trivial operation.

The second request (a list of all raw material requirements for finished assembly 7702), necessitates the finding of that record (tuple) in the Finished Assembly Relation and all raw materials listed therein. Any Subassemblies used also must be scanned for raw materials as well as the Component Part Relation. Obviously, the Purchased Part and Raw Material Relations need not be searched.

Although the relational model requires a fair amount of table searching, the operations themselves are simple and easy for a casual user to understand—certainly an advantage for many data processing environments.

A FEATURE ANALYSIS OF COMMERCIAL SYSTEMS

The features of the commercial systems to be reviewed here are only those discussed in this chapter: data manipulation language (DML), data definition language (DDL), and characteristics of the data model. These compose the major functional decision criteria for DBMS selection, but, of course, other features are important as well. Table 4.4 contains selected

FIGURE 4.5: Bill-of-Material Application Using the Relational Data Model

Finished Assembly Relation

A_1	A_2	A_3	A_4	$\cdots$	A_n
T_1					
T_2					
.					
.					
.					
T_m					

Subassembly Relation

A_1	A_2	A_3	A_4	$\cdots$	A_n
T_1					
T_2					
.					
.					
.					
T_m					

Component Part Relation

A_1	A_2	$\cdots$	A_n
T_1			
T_2			
.			
.			
.			
T_m			

Purchased Part Relation

A_1	A_2	A_3	$\cdots$	A_n
T_1				
T_2				
.				
.				
.				
T_m				

Raw Material Relation

A_1	A_2	A_3	$\cdots$	A_n
T_1				
T_2				
.				
.				
.				
T_m				

TABLE 4.4: Feature Analysis of Commercial Systems

System Name	Vendor	Cost (U.S. $)	DML	Standard	Data Model
ADABAS	Software AG of North America	2,000 per month	procedural nonprocedural	specialized	network
DATACOM/DB	Applied Data Research	37-44,000	procedural nonprocedural	specialized	relational-like
DBMS-10	Digital Equipment	30,000	procedural	CODASYL	network
DBMS-20	Digital Equipment	30,000	procedural nonprocedural	CODASYL	network
DL/I	IBM	395 per month	procedural	specialized	tree
DM/IV/ IDS-II	Honeywell	893 per month	procedural	CODASYL	network
DMS-II	Burroughs	23,000	procedural nonprocedural	specialized	network
DMS/90	Sperry Univac	no charge to Univac customers	procedural nonprocedural	CODASYL	network
DMS-1100	Sperry Univac	no charge to Univac customers	procedural nonprocedural	CODASYL	network

DPL	National Info Systems	23-38,000	procedural	specialized	tree and relational-like
DRS/XBS	A.R.A.P.	13-52,000	procedural	specialized	network
IDMS	Cullinane	45,000	procedural nonprocedural	CODASYL	network
IMS	IBM	646-950 per month	procedural nonprocedural	specialized	tree
INQUIRE	Infodata Systems	70-140,000	procedural nonprocedural	specialized	network and relational-like
MODEL 204	Computer Corporation of America	70-100,000	procedural	specialized	network and relational-like
RAMIS II	Mathematica Products Group	37,000	procedural nonprocedural	specialized	network and relational-like
SYSTEM 2000	MRI Systems	35,000	procedural nonprocedural	specialized	network and relational-like
TOTAL	Cincom Systems	18-57,000	procedural nonprocedural	specialized	network

features, primarily those covered in this chapter. Appendix A has the full range of characteristics specified for many commercial systems.

Note that a number of the commercial offerings include relational or relational-like systems. Although it is always true, based on theoretical descriptions, that one should be careful in selection, it is especially true for this class of system. In general, the relational or relational-like systems imply only that they use a tabular data model, not necessarily any sophisticated support software to assist in file normalization, which is typically necessary to avoid update and deletion anomalies that are well described by Codd [15].

SUMMARY OF CHAPTER CONTENTS

This chapter provides a number of taxonomies of DBMS characteristics. The standardized versus specialized approach was discussed. DML types from procedural to nonprocedural were compared. Data models consisting of chain, tree, network, and relational were presented. Finally, a feature analysis of commercially available systems was offered.

REFERENCES

1. R. G. Canning, "The Debate on Data Base Management," *EDP Analyzer* 10 (March 1972) 3.

2. R. G. Canning, "The Current Status of Data Management," *EDP Analyzer* 12 (February 1974) 2.

3. CODASYL, *Data Base Task Group Report,* (New York: Association for Computing Machinery, 1971).

4. V. K. M. Whitney, "Relational Data Management Implementation Techniques," *Proceedings of ACM-SIGMOD Workshop on Data Description, Access and Control* (1974): 321–48.

5. D. L. Waltz, "An English Language Question Answering System For A Large Relational Database," *Communications of the ACM* 21 (July 78) 7: 526–39.

6. G. D. Held and M. Stonebreaker, "Storage Structures and Access Methods in the Relational Data Base Management System INGRES," *Proceedings of ACM Pacific Regional Conference* (April 1975): 26–33.

7. G. D. Held, M. Stonebreaker and E. Wong, "INGRES—A Relational Data Base System," *Proceedings of the 1975 AFIPS National Computer Conference* 44 (1975): 409–16.

8. M. Stonebreaker, E. Wong, P. Kreps and G. Held, "The Design and Implementation of INGRES," *ACM Transactions of Database Systems* 1 (September 1976) 3: 189–212.

9. M. M. Astrahan and D. D. Chamberlin, "Implementation of a Structured English Query Language," *Communications of the ACM* 18 (October 1975) 10: 580–88.

10. M. M. Astrahan and R. A. Lorie, "SEQUEL-XRM, A Relational System," *Proceedings of ACM Pacific Regional Conference* (April 1975): 34–38.

11. W. Kim, "Relational Database Systems," *Computing Surveys* 11 (September 1979) 3: 185-211.

12. E. F. Codd and C. J. Date, "Interactive Support for Non-Programmers: The Relational and Network Approaches" (Paper delivered at ACM—SIGMOD Workshop on Data Description, Access and Control, Ann Arbor, Michigan, May 1-3, 1974).

13. C. J. Date and E. F. Codd, "The Relational and Network Approaches: Comparison of the Application Programming Interfaces" (Paper delivered at ACM-SIGMOD Workshop on Data Description, Access and Control, Ann Arbor, Michigan, May 1-3, 1974).

14. Charles W. Bachman, "The Programmer As Navigator," *Communications of the ACM* 16 (November 1973) 11: 653-58.

15. E. F. Codd, "Further Normalization of the Data Base Relational Model," *Data Base Systems: Courant Computer Science Symposia Series* 6, Englewood Cliffs, N.J.: Prentice-Hall, May 1971, pp. 65-98.

PART II

DATA BASE DESIGN

INTRODUCTION

Part I developed a sense for the capabilities and limitations of DBMS technology (Chapter 16 will have more regarding DBMS applicability under different sets of conditions). The purpose of Part II is to discuss the major issues underlying the initial, and often most important, step in data base management: data base design. To simplify the analysis of a number of complex topics, four chapters will be used: Chapter 5 will discuss the data base design topic, in general, and partition all issues into the categories of user requirements definition, logical support definition, and physical support definition, which will be covered in Chapters 6, 7, and 8, respectively.

5

DATA BASE DESIGN ACTIVITIES

INTRODUCTION

The success of any IPS is highly dependent on the quality of its initial design and the appropriateness of any maintenance and/or modifications occurring during the life of the system. In general, the design of a data base consists of the following tasks:

1. Determination of data definitions as seen by application programs (subschemas);
2. Specification of global data base definitions as seen by the DBMS (schemas);
3. Construction and maintenance of the data dictionary/directory;
4. Design of search strategies;
5. Choice of access mechanisms;
6. Selection of data compression techniques;
7. Definition of policies to avoid problems resulting from concurrent update; .
8. Structuring of data security controls, including encryption;
9. Determination of procedures for integrity control; and
10. Selection and use of design aids.

The efficient structure of the data base supporting the IPS is crucial. A recent empirical study by Clark and Hoffer [1] reported reductions of roughly 40 percent in data base operational costs through the application of certain design aids. Although this study involved a rather simple data base design problem, larger problems pose formidable barriers to even design-aided attempts. Intuitively, the desirability of data base design aids (DBDAs) for selecting the best design alternative, if one exists, for a particular problem does not need justification. Unfortunately, the literature has not provided many useful design aids. This section will attempt to draw together within a taxonomic framework those design aids that are both practical and effective for many of the classic data base design problems.

For the purpose of developing a taxonomy, DBDA is considered to be any procedure or method that performs or adds structure to the performance of the data base design activity. The next section will define the data base design activity and develop a taxonomy of support-aids.

A TAXONOMY OF DATA BASE DESIGN AIDS

The system for classification of DBDAs should meet the following objectives:

1. Identify the individuals who have developed DBDAs, so the material they produce can be easily monitored for applicability to existing and new problems;
2. Describe the available techniques for purposes of selection;
3. Relate these techniques to specific data base design elements in an attempt to simplify the identification and selection process;
4. Provide references to detailed descriptions of each DBDA; and
5. Estimate the operational difficulty of the techniques.

The most suitable approach to classification is to identify the various elements of data base design, such as defining data requirements or determining file access techniques, and to develop the classification system based on these design elements. If the design elements are properly selected, the analyst will be able to relate the problem to one or more of these and then identify the applicable design aids. It is believed that as the technology of data base management systems changes, this approach will be far more stable than would a listing of specific design problems that might confront the designer.

To develop a taxonomy of the data base design activity, the interface activities of systems analysis and design must also be considered. The following outline contains three essential activities in implementing systems requiring data base support: user requirements definition, logical definition, and physical support definition.

TAXONOMY OF THE DATA BASE DESIGN ACTIVITY

I. User Requirements definition (URD): Specifies characteristics of information to be presented to the user including:

   A. Entities - the subject of inquiry
   B. Attributes - characteristics of the subject
   C. Values - indication of extent for each attribute
   D. Time - denotes either point in time or range of time of value-currency

   This class of design items answers the following questions: (1) what data is to be included in the user logical data base and (2) the format of user data presentation.

II. Logical Support Definition (LSD): Defines logical procedures for derivation of information from the URD including:

   A. Data structures:
      Linear
      Tree
      Network
      Relational
   B. Transformations:
      Arithmetic
      Logical

   These items serve to, one, describe data relationships and keys, two, select the appropriate data model and, three, identify synonyms.

III. Physical Support Definition (PSD): Identifies the physical implementation scheme.

   A. Storage structures
      Data layouts (attribute clustering or partitioning)
      Access paths
   B. Procedures
      Access methods
      Data transformations
         Arithmetic
         Logical

   It is in this class of design activities that tradeoffs, primarily for efficiency or performance, are made.

User requirements definition specifies all required characteristics of information to be presented to the user. As such, it is only concerned with identification of entities, attributes, values, and the relevant point in time or range of time for the individual informational elements, as defined by Taggart [2].* In addition, because of training and/or limitations of systems design procedures, other noninformational elements may have to be specified by the user; for example, search key (selection criterion), sequence in which to present information (order criterion),† and either arithmetical or logical transformations.

Logical support definition identifies specific procedures for deriving the user requirements. To do this, two models must be selected: a data model and a transformation model. The data model logically establishes associations and potential access paths between attributes and must be navigated by the user's procedure, which also must be defined. The transformations to be performed are fully defined at this stage with due regard for appropriate data conversions from those that already exist in the data base.

Finally, implementation specifications occur in the physical support definition. Here, storage structures are laid out and physical data access and transformation procedures are specified.

There are numerous logical and physical factors that have an effect on the selection of alternative data base designs but over which the DBA does not have control. The staging of pages in different levels of a storage hierarchy is an example. If, however, the problem involves the selection of an appropriate storage area in the hierarchy for an attribute with certain use patterns, clearly, this is of concern to, and under the control of, the DBA. Therefore, discretion was necessarily used in the application of the taxonomy to the available literature.

The important dimensions of the DBDA taxonomy are input, process, output, and activity. Each dimension to be used in succeeding chapters of this section is described in the following paragraphs.

The input requirements of the various DBDAs often pose formidable problems to the user/designer; for the researcher, typically, they are assumed to be readily available. In general the input requirements fall into three categories: costs, operational statistics, and hardware/software characteristics. Costs of data storage and transfer are often traded off in arriving at good, if not optimal, data base designs. Operational statistics, such as attribute access probability or frequency of data base request submission, are also used in a large number of techniques to characterize the dynamics of the system. Finally, hardware/software characteristics provide the general bounds within which design alternatives must be selected; for

---

*Other possible classifications of informational elements are found in [3, 4, 5].

†See Severance [6] for a full definition of selection criterion and order criterion, among others.

example, storage capacity or latency delays are often fixed but must be considered during design so user requirements are met.

The class of solution techniques employed by the DBDA will determine the process dimension and has a significant effect on the level of difficulty involved in application. Each design aid will have the dimension coded according to the following scheme:

1. Descriptive Methodology (DM) may only contain general instructions or a step-by-step procedure for deriving a solution. Many ad hoc approaches to data base design would fall into this category.

2. Heuristic (H) is a procedure that completely defines all steps and may even guarantee optimal results.

3. Math Programming (MP) for which the procedure is completely specified guarantees optimal results (if all assumptions implicit in the model are met).

4. Closed-Form (CF) methods typically are applied to the more simplistic problems and may involve queueing theory.

The output of DBDAs is too varied to be strictly classified and remain useful. In addition, it is the primary factor of selection for the user/designer and, therefore, requires a high degree of precision in its statement. Each DBDA will have a short statement of the contents of its objective function (may be implied) made for this dimension.

Finally, the basic design activity addressed by the DBDA will be identified using the taxonomy of the Data Base Design Activity. Table 5.1 contains a summary of the relative attention that these general classes of problems have received both in literature and practice in terms of design aids.

TABLE 5.1: Summary of Relative DBDA Applicability to Design Activities

Design Activity	Number of Design Aids Covered	Percentage of Total
URD	4	7.6
LSD	16	30.9
PSD	32	61.5
	52	100.0

SUMMARY OF CHAPTER CONTENTS

This chapter defined a series of taxonomies for the selection of data base design aids. The design aids, which fall into the categories of URD, LSD, and PSD, will be treated separately in Chapters 6, 7, and 8.

REFERENCES

1. Jon D. Clark and Jeffrey A. Hoffer, "A Procedure for the Determination of Attribute Access Probabilities," *Proceedings of the 1978 ACM-SIGMOD International Conference on Management of Data,* Austin, Texas, May 31–June 2, 1978.

2. William M. Taggart, "Developing an Organization's Information Inventory," Working Paper 74-1, School of Business and Organizational Sciences, Florida International University, February 1974.

3. CODASYL Development Committee, "An Information Algebra Phase I Report," *Communications of the ACM* 5 (April 1962) 4: 190–204.

4. Borje Langefors, *Theoretical Analysis of Information Systems,* 4th ed. (Philadelphia, Penn: Auerbach Publishing, 1973).

5. Adrian M. McDonough and Leonard L. Garrett, *Management Systems: Working Concepts and Practices* (Homewood, Illinois: Richard D. Irwin, 1965).

6. D. G. Severance, "Some Generalized Modeling Structures for Use in Design of File Organizations" (Ph.D. dissertation, University of Michigan, 1972).

6

SOLUTION METHODOLOGIES FOR SELECTED USER REQUIREMENTS DEFINITION

INTRODUCTION

User requirements definition is typically under the purview of systems analysis and, as such, a complete discussion here is not only impossible but inappropriate. Nevertheless, a number of general statements can be made that are worthwhile regarding the output from this initial step in the data base design process. These will be followed by a taxonomy of URD techniques available and a brief description of one or more in each class.

The data base designer needs a variety of information to provide the user with effective and efficient systems; some originates from the user, some from the organization and its environment. The user can be thought of as having unbounded desires for information, perhaps even perfect information, whereas the organization and its environment places constraints on what can be provided in terms of computer support, data collected and retrieved, or simply the financial resources for systems design, implementation, and operation. The subject of this chapter is user requirements definition, which may or may not reflect consideration for these constraints. Nevertheless, the basis of any systems design and the construction of a user data base requires that certain basic parameters be provided. These consist of a definition of entity/attribute/value/time and, perhaps, some auxilliary requirements such as sequence, report or presentation format, currency, and timing.

The basic user requirement is the provision of information, which is defined in terms of one or more entity/attribute/value/time tuples (discussed in Chapter 2). How these are derived by the system is of no direct concern to the user, although many have been forced to consider such procedural details because of the lack of current system capability to do so directly from user specifications (more on this subject in Chapter 7). The remaining requirements determine to a large extent the usefulness of the information. The sequence in which data is presented and the format (for example, graphical, tabular, or prose) may have a tremendous effect on how easily (if not whether) information is absorbed by a user. This being the case, the user must be allowed to specify a preference or be offered alternatives.*

The required currency of the information provided, although subjected to the preferences of users, is primarily a function of the decisions to be made from the information. Table 6.1 depicts the currency and timing requirements characteristic of different levels of management.† Note that only information used for operational control purposes has extreme currency and timing requirements, whereas those of strategic planning are relaxed indeed.

TABLE 6.1: User Information Requirements by User Class

	Requirement	
User Class	Currency	Timing
Strategic planning	monthly-yearly	very long range
Management control	weekly-monthly	moderately long range
Operational control	up-to-the-minute-daily	immediate

A TAXONOMY OF URD TECHNIQUES

User requirements definition consists of defining only the essential elements of the information to be provided by an information system. As such, the entities, attributes, values, and time characteristic must be specified. The literature has addressed this problem, but, as can be seen from Table 6.2, not much attention has been paid to the subject.

User requirements definition can be accomplished in any of the following ways:

---

*See Mason and Mitroff [1] for a discussion of presentation mode types.
†Anthony's [2] typology is assumed here.

TABLE 6.2: User Requirements Definition Supported by the Literature

Activity	Number of Applicable Aids[a]
Entities	0
Attributes	4
Values	2
Time	1

[a]A single design aid may be relevant to more than one activity. Therefore, the total number of design aids may not be comparable between tables.

1. User definition;
2. User selection of classic model;
3. User/analyst dialogue; or
4. Analyst definition.

The first class, although the subject of considerable research [3–13], is not likely to be a commercial success for some time.* Training application users in systems analysis techniques is a partial solution but, for obvious reasons, not practical.

The second class of techniques involves the selection of a classic model for the system. Given that most systems have some precedent (that is, they are not original) then it is likely that a number of classic solutions exist. Consider accounts receivable or payable: These systems are so basic to the operations of public and private institutions that standard systems or solutions exist and can be purchased directly or built from published specifications. The problem with classic or standardized designs is that the user may have to accept slight compromises for the sake of generality. Nevertheless, this may be both less costly and expedient.

The third and fourth classes involve someone other than the decision maker lending a higher degree of expertise in general modeling, but less than adequate application-specific knowledge. For the third class, the user and an analyst create a dialogue; this is, in fact, the traditional method, using an application expert and a systems expert. Not too surprising is that virtually all general-purpose techniques available rely on this proven, but inexact, method. The fourth class, totally depending on an analyst, may result in classic or very naive models being selected.

---

*Several commercial products are available, including PSL/PSA, of the ISDOS project [9], and SADT, by Softech [7]. IBM's Query by Example [10, 11, 12, 13] permits the user to demonstrate informational requirements; but this is primarily suited for ad hoc queries, rather than frequently used batch systems.

The techniques of the first, second, and fourth classes, are too amorphous for discussion here. However, several techniques of the user/analyst dialogue type will be covered. In particular, those that are either automated or semiautomated will be discussed. All too frequently in data processing, DP technology is not applied to DP problems. The next section will discuss a number of techniques that rely on its application.

A DESCRIPTION OF SELECTED URD TECHNIQUES

The URD activity is very sparsely populated with design aids, as shown in Table 6.3. During the 1960s, IBM and NCR, respectively, developed the Time Automated Grid technique (TAG) [14] and Accurately Defined Systems (ADS) [15]. Both of these attempt to trace output requirements, as stated by the user but interpreted by an analyst, back to the constituent inputs, which might be present in the data base, while applying a variety of filtering mechanisms to insure accuracy, completeness, and consistency.

TABLE 6.3: Summary of User Requirements Definition Methodologies

Activity	Reference	Input	Process	Output
Attributes	Clark	Program code; or estimates of attribute use	DM	Required attributes
Attributes, values, time	IBM	Data input requirements; data output requirements	DM	Clean data requirements
Attributes, values	NCR	Report definition; input definition; computation description; history (file) specification; logic definition	DM	Accurate data requirements; key fields
Attributes	Teichroew & Hershey	System objects; relationships	DM	Accurate information requirements

FIGURE 6.1: Physical-to-Logical-Record Mapping Form

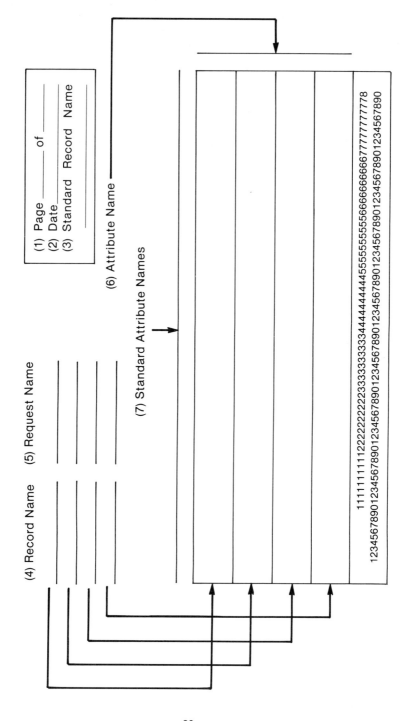

(1) Page _____ of _____
(2) Date _____
(3) Standard Record Name

(4) Record Name

(5) Request Name

(6) Attribute Name

(7) Standard Attribute Names

1111111111222222222233333333334444444444555555555566666666667777777778
1234567890123456789012345678901234567890123456789012345678901234567890

The ISDOS (Information System Design and Optimization System) project, too, has related, although more general, objectives, including the ultimate design and implementation of systems [9]. This system involving a Problem Statement Language (PSL) and a programmed Problem Statement Analyzer (PSA) insures accuracy, completeness, and consistency, and is commercially available.

Finally, the author has defined a relatively specialized technique [21, 22] for determining the necessary attributes to be included in the data base, assuming the availability of procedural descriptions of the application programs. Each of these techniques will be reviewed in moderate detail in the succeeding paragraphs.

A Procedure for Data Base Content Analysis

The author has defined a forms-driven procedure [21, 22] for data base content analysis that also assists in the determination of attribute access probabilities for logical and physical data base design methods. The author's procedure recognizes a variety of data use biases that confound the data base content analysis activity and that, therefore, lead to inefficient data base designs. The URD activity, however, requires an unbiased determination of data base content.

The filtering of attributes to be stored in the data base, so only those required are maintained from a practical point of view, is nontrivial. The author's procedure depends on an analysis of attribute use that is either estimated for new applications or derived directly from application programs. A set of four forms is used for this purpose.

The Physical-to-Logical-Record Mapping Form (Figure 6.1) assists in defining standard attribute names. By doing so, synonyms are identified and may be eliminated if desired. These standard attribute names will then be used throughout the analysis procedure. The form is structured as in most record layouts, but has room to describe four or more records (if multiple forms are used).

The Attribute Use Form (Figure 6.2) is applied to each request (program) and lists each standard attribute name and the program's reference for it (possibly a synonym), as well as the characteristic type of use that the attribute receives in the request. The use is of three classes: (I/O) from or to the data base, necessary use (U) within the request (that is, its appearance in an arithmetic or logical statement), and whether record selection (S) occurs as a result of that attribute.

The theory of this three-operation taxonomy of attribute use is that only attributes that originate in the data base and appear in arithmetic, logical, or selection-type statements are required for a given request. All others — those that receive just I/O or simply U or S-type use — are not

FIGURE 6.2: Attribute Use Form

(1)	Page _____ of _____
(2)	Date _____
(3)	Request Name
(4)	Standard Record Name
	_____

(5) Standard Attribute Name	(6) Attribute Name	(7) Use			(8) Set Membership
		I/O	U	S	

required. By applying this filtering mechanism, a surprising number of attributes can be removed from request access procedures. Whether an attribute is used as a selection criterion (SC), a projection schema (PS) or simply not required (NR), is recorded in the Set Membership column of the form.

The MOVE-Chain Form (Figure 6.3) is used to trace the use of attributes whose names change within a program. For example, if an attribute receives I/O use, is MOVED to another named area, then appears in a selection statement, clearly this must be recognized as a member of the selection criterion set. To do this, the use of the name employed for I/O and that for S must be consolidated. The consolidation occurs on attribute use forms as a result of the MOVEs recorded on the MOVE-Chain Form.

FIGURE 6.3: MOVE-Chain Form

(1)	Page _____ of _____
(2)	Date _____
(3)	Request Name
	_____

(4) Standard Attribute Name From	(5) Standard Attribute Name To

The Attribute Access Probability Form (Figure 6.4) is a summary document used to define the access probabilities for all standard attribute names of a request that have not been filtered out as a result of the analysis. By definition, all members of the selection criterion have an access probability of 1.00, and the projection schema members must have their probability estimated or calculated based on monitored data.

FIGURE 6.4: Attribute Access Probability Form

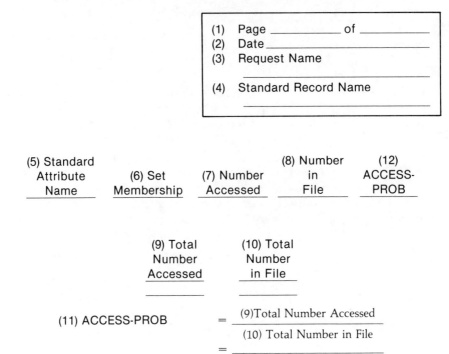

Although this technique, as with TAG and ADS, provides assistance at more than one level (for example, URD and LSD) its primary advantage, for the purpose of this chapter, is its ability to effectively and efficiently remove from request specifications attributes that are not required operationally, and that, if included in the data base design, would cause more costly operation.

Time Automated Grid Technique

TAG is a general-purpose-requirements specification and design aid for data processing systems developed and automated by IBM in 1966 [14]. Not only does it assist in structuring data collection, analysis of data requirements, and definition of data flow, but it does so with a single user/analyst collection instrument, a document called the Input-Output Analysis Form (Figure 6.5).

FIGURE 6.5: TAG's Input/Output Analysis Form

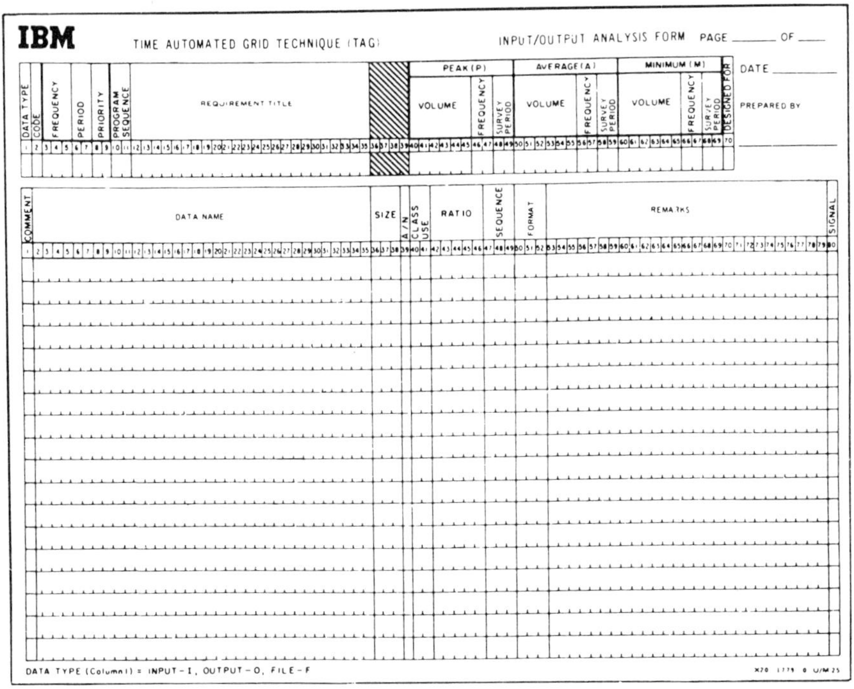
IBM TIME AUTOMATED GRID TECHNIQUE (TAG) INPUT/OUTPUT ANALYSIS FORM PAGE ____ OF ____

DATA TYPE | CODE | FREQUENCY | PERIOD | PRIORITY | PROGRAM SEQUENCE | REQUIREMENT TITLE | PEAK (P): VOLUME, FREQUENCY, SURVEY PERIOD | AVERAGE (A): VOLUME, FREQUENCY, SURVEY PERIOD | MINIMUM (M): VOLUME, FREQUENCY, SURVEY PERIOD | DESIGNED FOR

DATE ____ PREPARED BY ____

COMMENT | DATA NAME | SIZE | A/N | CLASS USE | RATIO | SEQUENCE | FORMAT | REMARKS | SIGNAL

DATA TYPE (Column 1) = INPUT - I, OUTPUT - O, FILE - F

Source: Courtesy of International Business Machines Corporation.

The form is broken into two sections, one describing characteristics of input; output; and any files being used, including frequency of use, period or time within which the data must be processed, and priority. The second section defines data requirements of the input, output, and files involved in the data processing task (for example, data name, its size, class of use, and ratio or relative frequency of data item use for each task run).

Although TAG is capable of producing ten reports for various uses, only those of major importance for data base are noted, as follows:

1. Glossary of Data-Names, including size, characteristics, and a reference number associated with each. This can be useful for standardization of terms and initialization of the DD/D.

2. Time-Grid Analysis facilitates the tracing of data element appearance, by time, through all data processing tasks. Intermediate files may be determined from this report.

3. Summary of Unresolved Conditions defines all data elements requiring further investigation for, among others, the following reasons: no input, not required to produce output, must be produced before some necessary input is available, and duplicates other data elements.

Although TAG is capable of supplying a useful variety of reports based on the user/analyst-supplied information from the Input/Output Analysis Form, it does have two serious shortcomings: although the information is contained in a single form it is nevertheless a complex one and requires a great deal of data collection and analysis prior to filling it out, and an unassisted user would not be capable of competently completing the forms.

TAG was never a commercial success, and it appears that its development was halted in midstream, prior to introduction. In a sense, this was unfortunate, because the information on the Input/Output Analysis Form would potentially drive a wide variety of design aids not only at the URD level but also at the LSD and PSD levels.

Accurately Defined Systems

A contemporary of TAG, ADS, developed by NCR in 1968 [15], takes a slightly different approach to the same general problem. Instead of relying on a single complex form for data collection, ADS employs a series of five specialized but simple documents. Although they are simple, an untrained user would be incapable of filling them out and, therefore, an analyst is required.

The Report Definition Form (Figure 6.6) consists of five sections: a fairly conventional printer layout, volume and triggering information for each line generated, crossreference of data to other source documents, sequencing data, and definition of selection rules for output.

Input Definition (Figure 6.7) is accomplished in two sections: a conventional 80-column format layout (multiples of 80 may be used) and field name specification, including size and validation rules, among others, followed by something called a "memo list," which provides an unstructured repository for such as descriptions and clarifications.

Computation Definition (Figure 6.8) describes all derived variables in terms of their constituent operands and operators, and provides a crossreference to the source (page and line) of each nonderived variable.

FIGURE 6.6: Report Definition

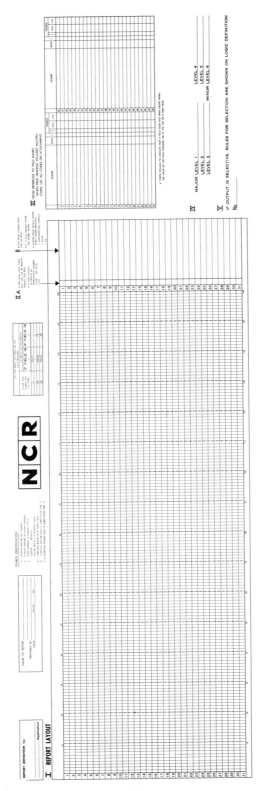

FIGURE 6.7: Input Definition

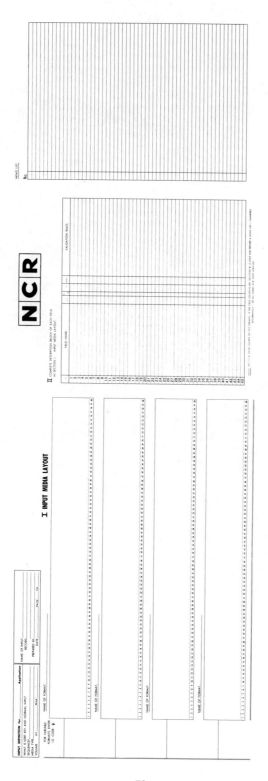

FIGURE 6.8: Computation Definition

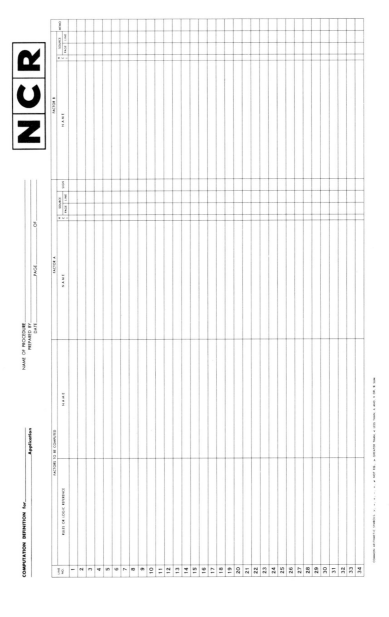

FIGURE 6.9: History Definition

HISTORY DEFINITION for_____Application	NAME OF GROUPING_____

NCR

PREPARED BY_____
DATE_____PAGE_____OF____

I FIELDS THAT IDENTIFY THIS HISTORY: _____

II WHAT IS THE EXPECTED VOLUME?   AV.   MAX.

III DESCRIBE EACH FIELD OF THE GROUP

Line No.	NAME	MEMO	% Occurs	A/N	Sign	Max. Size	How Long is Data Retained	See Note 1	SOURCE H C I	Page	Line
1											
2											
3											
4											
5											
6											
7											
8											
9											
10											
11											
12											
13											
14											
15											
16											
17											
18											
19											
20											
21											
22											
23											
24											
25											
26											
27											
28											
29											
30											
31											
32											
33											
34											
35											
36											
37											
38											
39											
40											
41											
42											
43											

NOTE 1 — EACH HISTORY FIELD ESTABLISHED WILL REQUIRE CHANGES
AND ADJUSTMENTS. A FIELD CHANGE CODE SHOULD BE
ASSIGNED IN THE INPUT SYSTEM FOR THIS PURPOSE. PLACE "✓" IN THIS COLUMN WHEN APPROPRIATE FIELD MAINTENANCE HAS BEEN PROVIDED.

FIGURE 6.10: Logic Definition

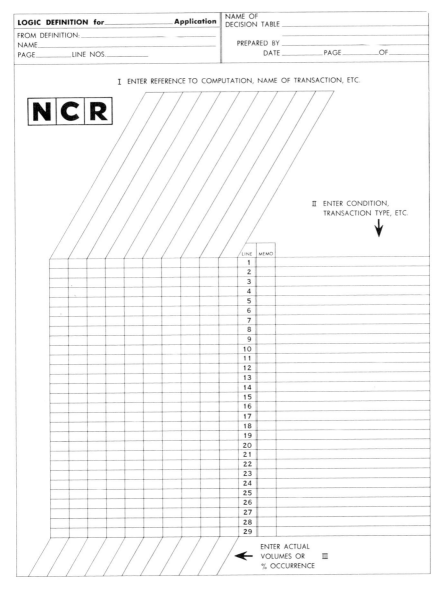

History Definition (Figure 6.9) is a description of a file consisting of its data contents, rules for coding, size of fields, retention of characteristics and, again, a page and line number for crossreferencing the source of each data element.

Logic Definition (Figure 6.10) is implemented in a decision-table format with specification of decision-rule frequencies so logic can be structured for efficiency.

The information contained on these forms permits the user (DBA) to trace all data from its source through any arithmetic or logical transformations to its ultimate use. A somewhat elaborate system of crossreferencing the flow of data from form to form is employed to facilitate this process. For the URD activity, this results in the description of a clean set of data requirements to be provided by the data base, without inconsistencies or ambiguities, and is, therefore, potentially a very useful tool. However, as with TAG the labor intensity of the technique is significant even for relatively simple systems definition. Once accomplished, though, generating systems designs and program development are greatly facilitated.

PSL/PSA

PSL/PSA is an outgrowth of the ISDOS project [3, 8, 9] headed by Daniel Tichroew at the University of Michigan. The ISDOS project originally set out to fully integrate the systems description, analysis, design, and implementation process. PSL/PSA primarily supports the description and analysis stages, and is one of the few currently supported commercially available systems for this purpose. Unlike TAG and ADS, both of which were early-generation methods, PSL/PSA does not rely on forms but is driven by a specialized language (PSL) that is in turn analyzed (compiled) by a software system (PSA).

Figure 6.11 depicts the operation of PSL/PSA. PSA depends on the support of a conventional computer operating system for its batch or on-line mode of operation. The command language controls the general operating characteristics of PSA. PSL serves as the user interface language and, as such, describes eight major aspects of any system to be analyzed:

1. System Input/Output Flow (interaction characteristics);
2. System Structure (for example, hierarchies);
3. Data Structure (relations among data);
4. Data Derivation (sources and uses of data);
5. System Size and Volume (factors influencing volume of processing);
6. System Dynamics (characteristics of system behavior);
7. System Properties (system objects); and
8. Project Management (for example, responsibilities and schedules).

FIGURE 6.11: Operation of PSL/PSA

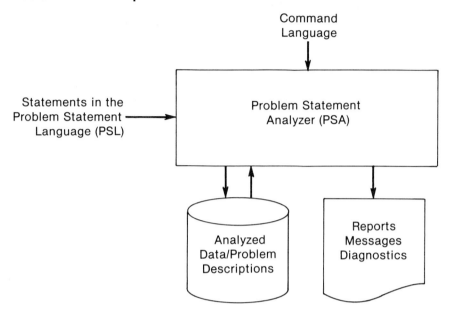

PSL provides a variety of types of objects and relationships which are used to describe these aspects. The PSA scans the descriptions provided in the PSL and begins to build a data base of acceptable data and systems descriptions, much like a DD/D. When errors or inconsistencies occur, or clarification is required, messages are output to the user. Reports are also produced including the following:

    1. Data Base Modification - record of changes to the data base
    2. Reference Reports - includes statement of the problem and contents of data base (DD/D - type information)
    3. Summary Reports - a wide variety are provided for project and data base management
    4. Analysis Reports - showing the behavior of the system, gaps in information flow, unused data, etc.

It should be obvious from the above description that PSL/PSA is useful for both URD and LSD activities. In addition, it is the only system described which has achieved a degree of commercial success. Though users have not claimed a reduction in development costs of systems as a result of it, it has dramatically affected the quality of the systems designed by it, particularly those of a very complex nature.

SUMMARY OF URD TECHNIQUES

The initial phase of systems analysis involves user requirement definition. Unfortunately, this has remained primarily an art, although attempts were made, beginning in the middle 1960s, to define procedures for facilitating URD and to apply data processing technology to the problem. This chapter surveyed a number of techniques including TAG, ADS, PSL/PSA, and one by the author that accomplish data base content analysis. The reason for the selection of these for presentation is two-fold: each is well documented in the literature, so additional information can easily be obtained; and together they demonstrate a philosophy of system description that has much in common. To be sure, there are other techniques worthy of study, including Structure Analysis and Design Techniques (SADT) by Softech [7].

REFERENCES

1. Richard O. Mason and Ian I. Mitroff, "A Program for Research on Management Information Systems," *Management Science* 19 (January 1973) 5: 475–87.

2. Robert Anthony, *Planning and Control Systems: A Framework for Analysis* (Cambridge, Mass.: Harvard University Press, 1965).

3. D. Teichroew and H. Sayani, "Automation of System Building," *Datamation* (August 1971): 25–30.

4. CODASYL Development Committee, "An Information Algebra Phase I Report," *Communications of the ACM* 5 (April 1962) 4: 190–204.

5. J. Katz and W. C. McGee, "An Experiment in Non-Procedural Programming," *Proceedings of AFIPS Fall Joint Computer Conference* (1963): 1–13.

6. Miles Hudson, *Automated Systems Technique (ASYST) System Description* NAVCOSSACT No. 91A019-TR01, Naval Command System Support Activity, Department of the Navy, Washington, D. C., Aug. 1969.

7. *An Introduction to SADT Structured Analysis and Design Technique* (Waltham, Mass.: SofTech, Inc., 1976).

8. Daniel Teichroew and Ernest Allan Hershey, III, "Computer-Aided Structured Documentation and Analysis of Information Processing System Requirements"(Paper presented at SHARE XLVII, Montreal, Canada, August 19, 1976).

9. Daniel Teichroew and Ernest A. Hershey, III, "PSL/PSA: A Computer-Aided Technique for Structured Documentation and Analysis of Information Processing Systems," *IEEE Transactions on Software Engineering* SE-3 (January 1977) 1: 41–48.

10. M. M. Zloaf, "Query-by-Example," *Proceedings of the National Computer Conference* 44 (1975): 431–38.

11. —— "Query-by-Example: A Data Base Language," *IBM Systems Journal* 16 (1977) 4: 324–43.

12. —— "Security and Integrity within the Query-by-Example Data Base Management Language," in *IBM Research Report RC 6982* (Yorktown Heights, New York: IBM Thomas J. Watson Research Center, 1978).

13. J. C. Thomas and J. D. Gould, "A Psychological Study of Query-by-Example," *Proceedings of the National Computer Conference* 44 (1975): 439–45.

14. IBM, "Time Automated Grid System (TAG). Sales and Systems Guide" White Plains, N. Y.: International Business Machines, Technical Publication GY20-0358-1, 2nd ed. (May 1971).

15. NCR, *A Study Guide for Accurately Defined Systems* (Dayton, Ohio: National Cash Register Co., 1968).

16. H. J. Lynch, "ADS: A Technique in Systems Documentation," *Data Base* 1 (Spring 1969) 1: 6–18.

17. O. T. Gatto, "Autostate," *Communications of the ACM* 7 (February 1964) 2: 425–32.

18. L. Lombardi, "A General Business-Oriented Language Based on Decision Expressions," *Communications of the ACM* 7 (February 1964) 2: 104–11.

19. C. B. B. Grindley, "SYSTEMATICS: A Non-Programming Language for Designing and Specifying Commercial Systems for Computers," *Computer Journal* 9 (August 1966): 124–28.

20. J. W. Young and H. Kent, "Abstract Formulation of Data Processing Problems," *Journal of Industrial Engineering* (November-December 1958): 471–79.

21. Jon D. Clark, "An Attribute Access Probability Determination Procedure" (Ph.D. dissertation, Case Western Reserve University, June 1977).

22. Jon D. Clark and Jeffrey A. Hoffer, "Physical Data Base Record Design." *Data Base Management* (Wellesley, Mass.: Q.E.D. Information Science, 1977) 7.

7

SOLUTION METHODOLOGIES FOR SELECTED
LOGICAL REQUIREMENTS DESCRIPTION

INTRODUCTION

Once the information to be presented to the user has been specified, the logical procedures for deriving the information from the data contained in the data base must be determined. For batch systems, the user typically doesn't care what procedures are used so long as the resulting information is correct. However, in on-line systems, the data model has a definite effect on the user's behavior and, therefore, this should be considered during application design.

The purpose of this chapter, as was that of Chapter 6, is to define a taxonomy of the logical requirements description activity and discuss a number of the techniques that support it. The decision criterion for determining which design aids to include in the chapter is generality of use; that is, only aids having general applicability will be discussed, although special purpose aids will also be given as references.

A TAXONOMY OF LOGICAL SUPPORT
DESCRIPTION METHODOLOGIES

Logical support definition (LSD) can be broken into two general areas: data structures and transformations. Data structures, of course, relate to the type of data model employed, and the set of possible models consists of linear, tree, network, and relational. These already have been discussed theoretically in Chapter 4. Data transformation, in general, consists of arithmetic and logical types. Arithmetic transformations may, for example, take some set of input values (for example, monthly sales) and derive an arithmetic mean (for example, average monthly sales). A logical transformation may be in the form of a decision table consisting of conditions and actions. The conditions present in a given situation are matched against those in the table; when a match is found the corresponding action is taken. Logical, rather than arithmetic, rules are involved here.

The literature has not paid equal attention to all areas of the LSD activity, as can be seen from Table 7.1. Although not intended to be an exhaustive sampling of design aids, there is a similar amount of activity in all data structure areas except for the linear category. This is not surprising, since the linear type of data structure is so limited in terms of usefulness and practicality that it doesn't warrant as much work. Note however, that within the transformation category logical methods dominate. Table 7.2 contains a brief description of the data base design aids applicable to the LSD activity.

TABLE 7.1: Logical Support Description Activity in the Literature

Activity	Number of Applicable Aids[a]
Data structures	3
Linear	0
Tree	3
Network	3
Relational	3
Transformations	1
Arithmetic	1
Logical	3

[a]A single design aid many be relevant to more than one activity; therefore, the total number of design aids may not be comparable between tables.

Logical system description has been the topic of numerous publications, particularly regarding data structures. Although many are specialized, there are three of general importance. Clark [1] offers a simple, yet effective, forms-driven technique for not only determining selection keys, but also for determining attribute access probabilities that are not subject to collection bias for the physical design problem that follows. Dearnly's [2] work depends on usage patterns and an access cost parameter, and provides the

TABLE 7.2:   Summary of Logical Support Description Methodologies

Activity	Reference	Input	Process	Output
Relational	Astrahan & Chamberlin [10]	Attributes, relations	H	Optimal accessing operations
Relational	Blasgen & Eswaran [11]	Access paths, physical clustering, query characteristics	DM	Minimizes accesses to secondary storage
Trees	Casey [4]	Query characteristics	H	Tree structures
Data structures	Clark [1]	Program code, or estimates of attribute usage, I/O volumes	DM	Access keys, attribute access probabilities
Trees	Coffman & Bruno [5]	Access frequencies, keys, length of file	H	Low search-time tree structures
Data structures	Dearnly [2]	Usage patterns, access cost	H	Optimal access technique
Networks	Gerritsen [7]	Query characteristics	H	Data structures, record contents, key fields
Relational	Hall [12]	Attributes, relations	H	Optimal sequence of relational impressions
Transformations: logical	IBM [13]	Data input requirements, data output requirements, activity ratios	DM	Clean logic requirements, unresolved conditions

(continued)

TABLE 7.2: (Continued)

Activity	Reference	Input	Process	Output
Data structures	Lum & Ling [3]	File character-istics, query statistics, fre-quency and speed of retrieval, space and time costs	MP	Tradeoff analy-sis for index selection
Transformations: arithmetic, logical	NCR [14]	Report defini-tion, input definition, com-putation description	DM	Accurate arith-metic and logi-cal require-ments
Trees	Patt [6]	Query charac-teristics	CF	Tree structures, storage re-quirements, average search length
Network	Raver & Hubbard [8]	Data element names, identi-fier, associa-tion type, fre-quency of use, nature of access	H	Determine re-quired associa-tions, define keys, relative measure of im-portance of access paths, candidates for secondary in-dexes
Transformations	Smith & Chang [15]	Query characteristics	H	Optimum per-formance pro-gram
Networks	Teichroew & Hershey [9]	System ob-jects, rela-tionships	DM	Complete and consistent logic definition
Transformations: logical (relational)	Wang & Wedekind [16]	Relations	H	Minimal cover set

user with an optimal logical access technique. In addition, this is a self-organizing tool that assists in determing physical record designs. The technique offered by Lum and Ling [3] provides an optimal solution to the problem of selecting the set of keys on which to index a file; this, of course, depends on a number of parameters, one of which, query statistics, could be collected using the procedure set out by Clark.

The typical problem addressed involving trees, a special case of data structures, is that of determining designs that result in low, if not minimal, search time. Both Casey [4] and Coffman and Bruno [5] have provided heuristics for this problem. Patt [6], on the other hand, offers a closed-form solution for minimizing average search time.

There are three methods reviewed for network applications. Gerritsen [7] has defined a nonprocedural language-driven design system that produces a minimal set of data structures including key fields and record contents. Raver and Hubbard [8] report on IBM's Data Base Design Aid, which is one of the only commerically available tools that actually prescribes a logical design. In doing so, it defines the required associations, keys, and secondary indexes, and calculates a parameter representing access path importance. Although it is a workable tool, it does not attempt to trade off the classic set of costs for data base operations, storage, and transfer costs. This may, however, be its strength since some techniques, although elegant and precise, are computationally infeasible. Because of the practical importance of this class of design methodologies, it is surprising that IBM is the only computer manufacturer offering such a tool. Teichroew and Hershey [9] have reported on PSL/PSA from the ISDOS project, which, in part, defines relationships among data but does not go further toward the physical design of the data base. This, too, is one of the few commercially available techniques, although quite expensive operationally.

The relational subcase of data structures has received a tremendous amount of attention; however, there are still very few data base design methodologies. Three of these methodologies are offered here, and relate to the minimization of accesses to secondary storage. Astrahan and Chamberlin [10] describe an interpreter for SEQUEL, which minimizes accessing operations for arbitrary queries. Blasgen and Eswaran [11] offer a set of relevant techniques, the choice of which is quite subjective. Nevertheless, the performance of these techniques is compared numerically and analytically. Hall [12] examines the optimization of a single query requiring little overhead.

Logical transformations are also necessary at this level of specification. Both IBM's Time Automated Grid [13] technique and NCR's Accurately Defined Systems [14], in part, trace the flows of all logical and arithmetic operations within systems; consistency and completeness are checked. It is significant that these methods also were applicable to URD, TAG, and PSD. Smith and Chang [15] offer a suggestion for supporting automatic programming tailored to a relational view of data. Wang and Wedekind [16] present an approach that removes redundant relations for logical data base design.

The next section will describe in detail several general techniques for the LSD activity.

A DESCRIPTION OF SELECTED LOGICAL SYSTEM DESCRIPTION TECHNIQUES

Three techniques have been selected for description in this section. An attempt was made to find an automated, or at least semiautomated, design aid that would be both efficient and effective for each of the basic data models except linear. Although there are many others for which references are provided, the selected techniques are by Patt [6] for tree structures, IBM (as discussed by Raver and Hubbard [8]) for networks, and by Blasgen and Eswaren [11] for the relational model.

A Design Aid for Tree Structures

The selected design aid for tree structures is that by Patt [6]; although ten years old, it remains quite useful. Recognizing that three structures are either of the fast-search/slow-update or slow-search/fast-update type, unless doubly chained—one chain for each type of use—a procedure is developed for constructing a tree with a minimum average search time. Although too complex for complete presentation, here are several equations of interest. The equations are a closed-form expression for minimum average search time as a function of the number of terminal modes, storage capacity required to support the doubly chained tree structure, and the total cost of the structure (using Sussenguth's [17] cost criterion).

The necessary variables are as follow:

$Pr(j)$ = the position within its filial set of the node on the rth level in the path to the terminal node j

$h(j)$ = the level of the tree on which node j appears

$m = \sum\limits_{r=1}^{h(j)} Pr(j)$ the search length of a node j, which is proportioned the to number of nodes queried, from the left-most root to the terminal node

N = number of terminal nodes

There are two general cases for adding a new terminal node (hence generating a new design) to a tree structure:

Case 1—where $2^m \leqslant N < (3/2)2^m$.

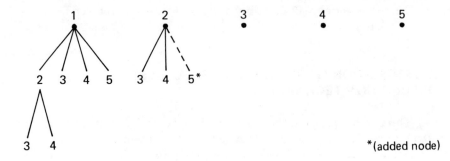

*(added node)

Case 2—where $(3/2)2^m \leqslant N < 2^{m+1}$.

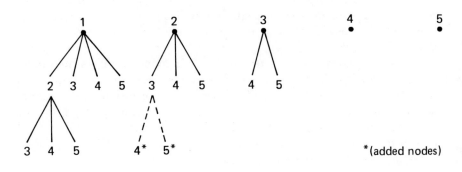

*(added nodes)

The closed-form expression for minimum average search time $\bar{t}(N)$ as a function of the number of terminal modes N is as follows:

For the case $2^m \leqslant N \leqslant (3/2)\ 2^m$ (Case 1):

$$\bar{t}(N) = m + 2 - \frac{3 \times 2^{m-1}}{N}$$

For the case $(3/2)2^m \leqslant N \leqslant 2^{m+1}$ (Case 2):

$$\bar{t}(N) = m + 3 - \frac{3 \times 2^m}{N}$$

These equations could effectively be used to estimate either relative search times of various tree structures or absolute times, if the machine instruction times for each node search were known. The data base designer would, therefore, be able to select the least costly structure, based on time.

The storage capacity, $f(N)$, required to support this class of tree structures is:

For the case $2^m \leqslant N \leqslant (3/2)2^m$ (Case 1):

$$f(N) = N + 2^{m-1} - 1$$

For the case $(3/2)2^m < N \leqslant 2^{m+1}$ (Case 2):

$$f(N) = 2(N - 2^{m-1}) - 1$$

If storage space is either costly or restricted, these equations will assist in identifying the alternative with the least storage capacity requirement.

The minimum total cost of the structures, $C(N)$, according to Sussenguth [17] is

$$C(N) = 3.88 \, (N-1) \log_{5.3} N$$

or, for large N approaches,

$$C(N_{large}) = 1.64 \, N \log_2 N$$

This considers both search time and storage capacity requirements, and is a relative measure only, the minimum cost being unity.

In total, the equations provided by Patt serve as relatively effective estimators of operational efficiency for data structures involving trees. In addition, the data collection requirements are quite reasonable, considering the design assistance they provide.

A Design Aid for Network Structures

Raver and Hubbard [8] have presented the details of one of the few automated data base design aids by IBM (called Data Base Design Aid). In general, Data Base Design Aid sets out to do the following:

1. Identify homonyms and synonyms;
2. Detect many types of inconsistencies and incompletely defined requirements;
3. Identify and eliminate inessential access paths; and
4. Provide a rigor on data gathering and analysis that otherwise would not exist, thus reducing errors, omissions, and inconsistencies.

As with any LSD technique, associations among data are important. Data Base Design Aid recognizes three basic types: a simple association (Type 1) in which each occurrence of one element identifies one, and only one, occurrence of another (thus, simple mapping); complex association (Type M) where any occurrence of an element can identify one or more elements (a one to many relation); and a conditional association (Type C) where the "from" element may or may not identify a "to" element. By classifying all application associations according to this scheme, one can then begin to combine application views into a single, global network of nonredundant elements and their associations. Edits for errors, omissions, and inconsistencies, elimination of inessential associations, and identification of keys and attributes are then performed, with the designer assisted by diagnostic and design reports. Figure 7.1 depicts Data Base Design Aid's operation.

Although the input requirements are modest enough, the reports are what interest the data base designer. The Parent/Child Graph is derived from the Structural Model and represents the physical hierarchical structures of the data base. Suggested Segments including key name, attribute names, specification of fixed or variable lengths, and segment size are also provided. The Structured Model shows all possible parent/child relationships in network form and a summary of the association weights for each path. This association weight may be used to select the access paths to be supported. A report of Candidates for Secondary Indexes is provided to identify those elements that appear as a root in the requirements of some applications, but not as a root in the suggested hierarchical structure; these are candidates for secondary indexes. Finally, a report of Association Weights can be used to select access paths. In some cases, batch and on-line requirements may be identified separately, as well as special weighting of insertions, replacements, and deletions.

The initial field experience with IBM's Data Base Design Aid indicates that it does have an effect on the quality of the design activity, and shortens the design and implementation process.

A Design Aid for Relational Structures

Relational data base has received much attention in the literature, including a number of data base design aids [10, 11, 12, 16]. The design aid

FIGURE 7.1: Operation of a Data Base Design Aid

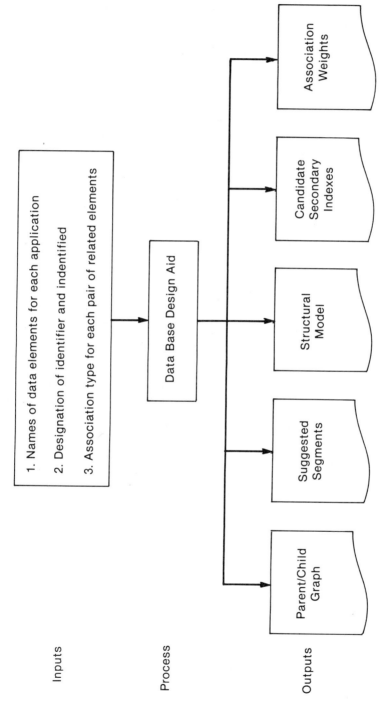

Inputs

1. Names of data elements for each application

2. Designation of identifier and indentified

3. Association type for each pair of related elements

Process

Data Base Design Aid

Outputs

Parent/Child Graph

Suggested Segments

Structural Model

Candidate Secondary Indexes

Association Weights

Source: Courtesy of International Business Machines Corporation.

87

to be covered here is one by Blasgen and Eswaran [11]. The decision methodology provides both analytical and numerical comparisons of four retrieval techniques with regard to the cost of accessing secondary storage.

The general query requiring processing involves the relational operators of restriction, projection, and join. For example, a given set of restrictions may be applied to relations R and S yielding R^1 and S^1. The join operation may then be applied to R^1 and S^1 to form a new relation, T, which will have a subset of its columns projected for the user.

The issue dealt with in this methodology is which, of the four access models, should be selected under different sets of operational conditions. The four access models are as follow:

1. Indexes in join columns: Indexes for the join columns of R and S are scanned to find identical values. If any are found, they are checked for satisfaction of the corresponding restrictions. All such tuples are put into temporary storage, which must be sufficiently large to hold the maximum number of restricted subtuples. Ultimately, the subtuples of interest are projected.

2. Sorting both relations: The relations R and S are scanned; and files are created containing subtuples of each corresponding to tuples, R(S), that satisfy the predicate. These files are then joined on the column values after having been sorted.

3. Multiple passes: The tuples of S are obtained by a scan. Provided the access path is not the restriction column index, the restriction is applied as each tuple is encountered. Qualified tuples are projected, and if there is space in main storage, resulting subtuples are inserted in the data structure. If there is no space, and if the join column values in S are less than the current highest join column value in the data structure W, the subtuples with the highest join value in W are deleted and S inserted. If there is no room for S and the join value in S is greater than the highest in W, S is not inserted at all. Once W is formed, R is scanned for tuples satisfying the predicate. Then W is checked for the presence of a join column value for that tuple, and if matched, are joined to the corresponding subtuples in W.

4. Simple tuple identifier: Using restriction column indexes, relevant tuple identifiers are obtained, sorted, and stored in files R^1 and S^1. The join column indexes are scanned and the tuple identifiers for the joins are found. If the identifiers are found in both R^1 and S^1, they are fetched and joined, and the relevant subtuple is obtained.

These four methods were then evaluated by Blasgen and Eswaran under three situations and four levels of predicate filtering. The situations tested were:

A. Join column indexes, and indexes of irrevelant columns X and Y exist. R and S are clustered on columns X of R, and Y of S.

FIGURE 7.2: Comparison of the Costs of the Applicable Methods in Situation A

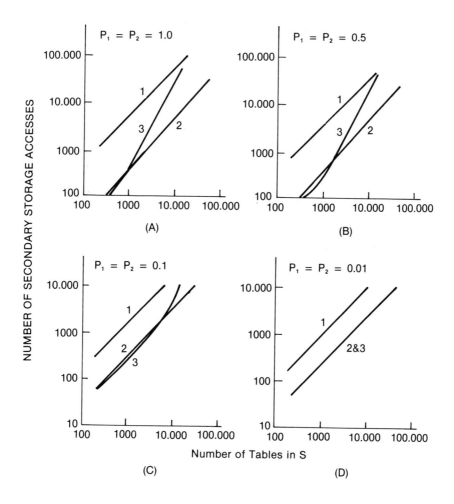

Source: Courtesy of International Business Machines Corporation.

FIGURE 7.3: Comparison of the Costs of the Applicable Methods in Situation B

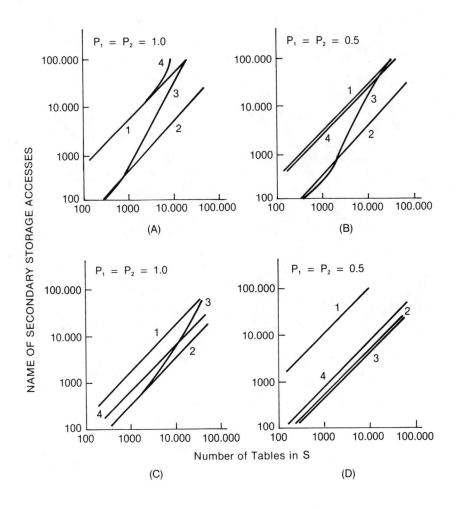

Source: Courtesy of International Business Machines Corporation.

FIGURE 7.4:   Comparison of the Costs of the Applicable Methods in Situation C

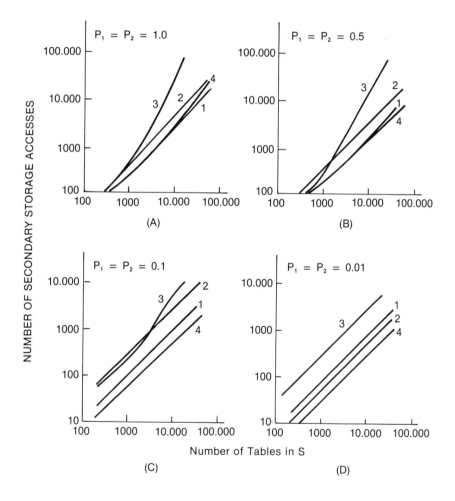

Source: Courtesy of International Business Machines Corporation.

B. Join column indexes, restriction column indexes, and indexes on irrelevant columns X and Y exist. R and S are clustered on columns X and Y.

C. Join column indexes and indexes on the restriction columns exist. R and S are clustered only on the join column indexes.

For each situation there will be a set of four different sensitivities of predicate filtering; the sensitivity is the ratio between the number of tuples that satisfy the predicate and the cardinality of the relation. Figures 7.2, 7.3, and 7.4 depict the performance of the four techniques under three sets of conditions and four filtering sensitivities.

As noted by Blasgen and Eswaran, and shown in the figures, each of the methods is best under certain conditions and the cost difference between the best two is, in most situations, significant.

SUMMARY OF LSD TECHNIQUES

Logical system description has received much more attention in the literature and practice than has the URD activity. This is primarily because of computer science and the general applicability of mathematics to many of the problems faced at this level of analysis. This chapter presented design techniques for the three major data models: those described by Patt [6], Raver and Hubbard [8], and Blasgen and Eswaran [11] for trees, networks, and the relational model, respectively. Although transformation (arithmetic and logical) design aids exist, they have not been covered, but references for them have been provided.

REFERENCES

1. Jon D. Clark, "An Attribute Access Probability Determination Procedure" (Ph.D. dissertation, Case Western Reserve University, 1977).

2. P. Dearnly, "A Model of a Self-Organizing Data Management System," *The Computer Journal* 17 (1974): 13–16.

3. V. Y. Lum and H. Sing, "An Optimization Problem on the Selection of Secondary Keys," *Proceedings of the 26th National Conference, ACM* (1971): 349–56.

4. R. G. Casey, "Design of Tree Structures for Efficient Querying," *Communications of the ACM* 16 (1973) 9: 549–56.

5. E. G. Coffman and J. Bruno, "On File Structuring for Non-Uniform Access Frequencies," *Nordisk Behandlings Information Tedskrift* 10 (1970): 443–56.

6. Yale M. Patt, "Variable Length Tree Structures Having Minimum Average Search Time," *Communications of the ACM* 12 (1969) 2: 72–76.

7. Rob Gerritsen, "A Preliminary System for the Design of DBTG Data Structures," *Communications of the ACM* 18 (1975) 10: 551–57.

8. N. Raver and G. U. Hubbard, "Automated Logical Data Base Design: Concepts and Applications," *IBM Systems Journal* 16 (1977) 3: 287–312.

9. D. Teichroew and E. A. Hershey, "PSL/PSA: A Computer-Aided Technique for Structured Documentation and Analysis of Information Processing Systems," *IEEE Transactions on Software Engineering* SE-3 (1977) 1: 41–48.

10. M. M. Astrahan and D. D. Chamberlin, "Implementation of a Structured English Query Language," *Communications of the ACM* 18 (1975) 10: 580–88.

11. M. W. Blasgen and K. P. Eswaran, "Storage and Access in Relational Data Base," *IBM Systems Journal* 16 (1977) 4: 363–77.

12. P. A. V. Hall, "Optimization of Single Expressions in a Relational Data Base System," *IBM Journal of Research and Development* (May 1976): 244–57.

13. IBM, "Time Automated Grid Systems (TAG): Sales and Systems Guide." White Plains, N.Y.: International Business Machines, Technical Publication GY20-0358-1, 2nd ed. (May 1971).

14. NCR, *A Study Guide for Accurately Defined Systems.* (Dayton, Ohio: National Cash Register Co., 1968).

15. John Miles Smith and Philip Yen-Tang Chang, "Optimizing the Performance of a Relational Algebra Interface," *Communications of the ACM* 18 (1975) 10: 568–79.

16. C. P. Wang and H. H. Wedekind, "Segment Synthesis in Logical Data Base Design," *IBM Journal of Research and Development* (January 1975): 71–77.

17. E. H. Sussenguth, Jr., "Use of Tree Structures for Processing Files," *Communications of the ACM* 6 (May 1963) 5: 272–79.

8

SOLUTION METHODOLOGIES FOR SELECTED PHYSICAL SUPPORT DEFINITION

INTRODUCTION

Chapters 6 and 7 have discussed methodologies for defining user information requirements and logical procedures by which these elements may be retrieved or derived. Because of the high cost of hardware, although the cost is decreasing with time, efficiency problems must be addressed. Simply choosing any workable physical solution to data storage and retrieval is not tolerable. Efficient physical designs must be derived so the costs of information systems remain within reasonable limits. Techniques for this purpose have dominated the computer science literature for years, and it is the purpose of this chapter to classify them and to present several general purpose and useful design aids. As in Chapters 6 and 7, only a few will be discussed in detail, but references, with a brief description, to a much larger set will be provided.

A TAXONOMY OF PHYSICAL SUPPORT DEFINITION METHODOLOGIES

A taxonomy of physical support definition (PSD) might consist of techniques for storage structures, and another class for procedures. Storage structure design aids, on the one hand, typically fall into two categories:

those for data layout, which are most commonly found in the literature; and those for access path design. Procedures, on the other hand, fall into the categories of access methods and data transformation, which latter consists of arithmetic and logical types.

As can be seen from Table 8.1, data layout design aids dominate the literature, followed by access path and access method techniques.

TABLE 8.1: Physical Support Definitions in the Literature

Activity	Number of Applicable Aids[a]
Storage Structures	1
Data Layouts	20
Access Paths	5
Procedure	0
Access Methods	4
Data Transformations	1
Arithmetic	1
Logical	0

[a]A single design aid may be relevant to more than one activity; therefore, the total number of design aids may not be comparable between tables.

Table 8.2 contains brief descriptions of the design aids that fall into these categories of the PSD activity.

By far the greatest attention has been paid to the PSD activity; it is this area that contains the most solvable problems. Two words of caution are in order for methods of this class: one, many techniques require parameter values that, at best, are difficult to obtain but may dramatically affect the resulting solutions and, two, methods using either heuristics or math programming may have questionable computational feasibility when applied to problems of realistic size.

Most of the techniques surveyed are specialized. Senko, Lum, and Owens [1], however, offer one with more universal applicability for estimating processing time, based on descriptions of queries to be serviced, file content, and organization.

TABLE 8.2: Summary of Physical Support Definition Methodologies

Activity	Reference	Input	Process	Output
Data layout	Babad [2]	Storage characteristics, storage costs, transfer costs,access probabilities, use characteristics	MP	Record partitions, file partitions
Data layout	Benner [9]	Data activity, storage characteristics, probability of field occurrence, length of control fields	H	Size of main physical record, improved storage use
Access paths	Bloom [24]	Number of records in data base, hardware characteristics, query characteristics	DM	Retrieval time characteristics
Access methods	Cardenas [28]	Storage characteristics, access times, data file characteristics	DM	Index keys, access time, storage requirements, index organization, search method
Data layout	Cardenas [14]	Storage costs, storage characteristics, access time, update costs, hardware characteristics	DM	Storage costs, access times
Data layout	Chandy & Ramamoorthy [15]	Cost constraint, activity profile	MP	Minimum access time

(continued)

TABLE 8.2: (Continued)

Activity	Reference	Input	Process	Output
Access paths	Chow [22]	Number of attributes, bucket size	CF	Balance file organizations
Data layout	Chu [20]	Storage cost, transmission cost, file length, request rates, access time, storage capacity	MP	Minimizes overall operating cost (storage and transmission)
Data layout	Clapson [16]	File capacity, file load percentage, bucket size	DM	Average number of records, maximum number of accesses to locate a record
Access paths	Collmeyer & Shemer [25]	File organization, storage device characteristics	CF	Mean retrieval time
Data layout	Dearnly [3]	Use patterns, access cost	H	File designs
Data layout	Eisner & Severance [4]	Storage costs, transfer costs, data item lengths, retrieval patterns	MP	Optimum segmentation of records
Data layout	Hoffer [5]	Storage costs, transfer costs, access probabilities, use characteristics, hardware characteristics	MP	Optimal clusters of attributes (possible redundancy), optimal partitions of attributes (no redundancy)

(continued)

TABLE 8.2: (Continued)

Activity	Reference	Input	Process	Output
Data layout	IBM [6]	Data input requirements, data output requirements, activity ratios	H	Record structures
Access methods	Lum [28]	Number of values in index, number of fields in query	DM	Number of accesses, storage requirements
Access methods	Lum, Ling, & Senko [29]	Number of index links, physical location of index and data, block size, overflow size and placement, number of buffers, transaction volume, file size, record size	DM	Characteristics of selected link access methods
Data transformation (arithmetic)	Lum, Yuen, & Dodd [32]	Load factor, bucket size	H	Transformation technique, average number of acesses per record, number of overflow records, overflow handling technique
Data transformation	Maxwell & Severance [31]	Attribute value length, length of control field, length of control list	CF	Optimal representation of attribute values

(continued)

TABLE 8.2: (Continued)

Activity	Reference	Input	Process	Output
Data layout	Milman [10]	File size, average length, average access per retrieval	CF	Optimal storage space
Data layout	Rothnie & Lozano [7]	Number of records, number of pages, number of attributes, access probabilities	H	Optimum clustering of records
Data layout	Schkolnick [8]	Data relationships, physical device characteristics	MP	Optimal partitions of elements to minimize access time, may also determine costs of alternatives
Data layout	Shneiderman [17]	Access costs, reorganization cost, rate of deletions, number of overflows, size and number of records	CF	Optimum reorganization points
Access methods	Senko, Ling, Lum, Meadow, Bryman, Drake, & Meyer [30]	Number of index links, physical location of index and data, block size; overflow size and placement, number of buffers, transaction volume, file size, record size	DM	Characteristics of selected link access methods

(continued)

TABLE 8.2: (Continued)

Activity	Reference	Input	Process	Output
Storage structures	Senko, Lum & Owens [1]	Query and update transaction descriptions, file content and organization description	DM	Estimates processing time
Access paths	Severance & Carlis [23]	Quantity of records retrieved, speed of response, volume of on-line update	DM	Access paths
Date layout	Severance & Merten [11]	Physical characteristics of data, characteristics of storage medium, data volatility	DM	Space, maintenance, and retrieval parameters for a variety of alternative designs
Access paths	Siler [26]	Response time characteristics, number of records per bucket, storage device characteristics, queueing probabilities	H	Access times
Data layout	Tuel [18]	Cost of access, life of file	MP	Optimum reorganization intervals
Data layout	van der Pool [12]	Storage characteristics, storage costs, file activity, access costs	CF	Bucket size

(continued)

TABLE 8.2: (Continued)

Activity	Reference	Input	Process	Output
Data layout	van der Pool [21]	Storage costs, file activity, access costs, storage characteristics	CF	Minimum retrieval cost
Data layout	van der Pool [13]	Storage characteristics, storage costs, file activity, access costs	CF	Bucket size
Data layout	Yao, Das & Teorey [19]	Search cost, reorganization cost	H	Near optimal reorganization points

Physical data layout has historically been of interest, although one wonders when the declining cost of storage will put a damper on further activity in this area. Twenty techniques were surveyed in this category. The partitioning or clustering of attributes into physical records has been well addressed by Babad [2], Dearnly [3], Eisner and Serverance [4], Hoffer [5], IBM [6], Rothnie and Lozano [7], and Schkolnick [8], and covers the range from simple decision methodologies to math-programming solutions. Storage size problems, too, have received attention, notably by Benner [9], Milman [10], Severance and Merten [11], and van der Pool [12, 13]. These methods cover the entire spectrum from decision methodology to closed-form solution. Cardenas [14], Chandy and Ramamoorthy [15], and Clapson [16] have covered access time problems, as these are frequently important in real-time systems. Perhaps the area requiring the most attention is that of determining when to reorganize the data base. Shneiderman [17], Tuel [18], and Yao, Das, and Teorey [19] have provided some initial work on the subject. Finally, the subject of operational cost of a system, although covered in many methods, is explicitly analyzed by Chu [20], and van der Pool [21].

The access path area is dominated by two types of problems: selection of the access path to use and the retrieval time to be expected. Chow [22], and Severance and Carlis [23] have offered solutions to the first problem. Bloom [24], Collmeyer and Shemer [25], and Siler [26] have provided solutions to the latter.

The second major division of the PSD activity consists of procedures for accessing data and making data transformations. This is a sparsely populated division. Cardenas [27]; Lum [28]; Lum, Ling, and Senko [29]; and Senko, et al. [30] have presented decision methodologies that evaluate various types of access procedures.

Maxwell and Severance [31] and Lum, Yuen, and Dodd [32] have offered solutions to the data transformation problem. Considering the wide variety of ways in which data may be coded, and the resulting effect on storage and transfer costs, it is surprising that more work has not been done on this topic.

From this cursory review of the work done in these specialized areas, we move, in the next section, to a number of general techniques for the PSD activity.

DESCRIPTION OF SELECTED PHYSICAL SUPPORT DEFINITION TECHNIQUES

Three general techniques have been selected for examination in detail. The first, by Hoffer [5], is a very effective and low operational overhead method for clustering attributes into physical records. It is simple, to the degree that only several parameters need be supplied by the user, and interpretation of the results is relatively straightforward. The second technique offered is a procedure for selecting record access paths, developed by Severance and Carlis [23]. This method also places very little data collection burden on the data base designer, and yet is quite effective for this important problem. Finally, a technique by Shneiderman [17] formalizing the data base reorganization problem is presented. Although more difficult to use (employ operationally), it nevertheless represents one of the few attempts reported in the literature to find a solution.

Physical Record Design

The clustering of data base attributes into physical records can be done by using a number of algorithms provided in the literature. Some, however, to insure optimality, require a great deal of computation and may as a result be impractical for problems of realistic size. One technique with an almost trivial computational burden, but with very useful output, is that by Hoffer [5], based on cluster analysis.

Hoffer has adapted the bond energy algorithm (BEA) developed by McCormick, et al. [34] for use in deriving an attribute similarity measure such that uses of similar attributes of a data base will be grouped together in a common subfile consisting of physical records. The similarity measure used by BEA depends on the following user-defined variables:

1. Probability of coaccess for each attribute;
2. Encoded length of attribute values;
3. Frequency of submission of each request;

4. Parameter β, which specifies the relative importance of value modification requests (VMRs) and read-only requests (RORs); and

5. General tuning parameter, α.

The output of BEA is a matrix with axes that identify the attribute and contains the similarity measure. If the similarity measure is high (that is, close to 1.00) then its use is very similar to the corresponding attribute. Low values (approaching 0.00) indicate highly dissimilar use patterns. The matrix, which is symmetric around the diagonal, indicates the similarity of Attribute One's use with Attribute One, Two with Two, etc.; hence, the values on the diagonal are 1.00.

Table 8.3 contains an example matrix from BEA, the interpretation of which is subjective. The data base designer must cluster the attributes contained in the matrix into a suitable number of groups; typically, the number corresponds to the number of physical areas independently addressable by the computer system. In the case of Table 8.3 assume three areas are available. Ideally, the designer will find clusters of similar values that can be segregated into a single physical area for purposes of storage and transfer. Note how Cluster One, consisting of Attributes One-Four, has similarity values ranging from 0.75 to 0.92 (neglecting the diagonal); Cluster Two, consisting of Attributes Five-Nine, ranging from 0.38 to 0.55; Cluster Three, containing Attributes Ten-Twelve, has similarity values ranging from 0.10 to 0.32. If two areas were available to the designer, then some other arbitrary set of similarity value cutoff points would be employed.

Naturally, it is very unlikely that the clusters would be so apparent. Several designers might well describe different clusters. Nevertheless, it has been shown by Hoffer [5] that the range of clusters chosen by several data base designers will perform in a similar fashion with one another.

Selection of Record Access Paths

There are a number of feasible alternatives to any physical record access problem. The selection of the most appropriate, for a given application, is important for the success of the system; therefore, a reliable selection technique is needed to assist the data base designer. Severance and Carlis [23] have defined a heuristic approach to this problem. In Table 8.4 they present performance characteristics for a range of commonly found record search techniques based on mathematical models available in the literature [35]. As can be seen, the relative performance of the techniques varies widely. However, if calculated for different file sizes, the relative speeds may well change.

Other operational conditions affect selection, and Severance and Carlis have chosen the following parameters to drive their heuristic: speed of

TABLE 8.3: Attribute Use Similarity Matrix Attributes

	1	2	3	4	5	6	7	8	9	10	11	12
1	1.00	0.80	0.75	0.85	0.50	0.47	0.52	0.40	0.55	0.29	0.35	0.18
2	0.80	1.00	0.92	0.78	0.54	0.52	0.39	0.45	0.50	0.22	0.25	0.24
3	0.75	0.92	1.00	0.88	0.38	0.45	0.42	0.50	0.48	0.20	0.18	0.30
4	0.85	0.78	0.88	1.00	0.40	0.52	0.42	0.45	0.48	0.28	0.10	0.15
5	0.50	0.54	0.38	0.40	1.00	0.39	0.45	0.48	0.40	0.17	0.19	0.20
6	0.47	0.52	0.45	0.52	0.39	1.00	0.49	0.51	0.53	0.19	0.15	0.28
7	0.52	0.39	0.42	0.42	0.45	0.49	1.00	0.49	0.43	0.30	0.15	0.20
8	0.40	0.45	0.50	0.45	0.48	0.51	0.49	1.00	0.41	0.25	0.23	0.30
9	0.55	0.50	0.48	0.48	0.40	0.53	0.43	0.41	1.00	0.32	0.18	0.18
10	0.29	0.22	0.20	0.28	0.17	0.19	0.30	0.25	0.32	1.00	0.20	0.22
11	0.35	0.25	0.18	0.10	0.19	0.15	0.15	0.23	0.18	0.20	1.00	0.14
12	0.18	0.24	0.30	0.15	0.20	0.28	0.20	0.30	0.18	0.22	0.14	1.00

TABLE 8.4: Performance Characteristics for Common Record Search Techniques

Search Technique	Theoretical Average Number of Comparisons for N Records	Statistics Typical for 50,000 Employee Records		
		Average Number of Comparisons	Search Time (in seconds)	Space Overhead (in percent)
Scanning	$(N + 1)/2$	25000	50	0
Direct Addressing	1	1	0.1	500
Binary Search	$\log_2(N/2)$	15	1.5	0
Tree Search	$1.4 \log_2 N$	22	2.2	3-5
Full Index	$(N + 1)/2$	25000	3-6	3-8
Block Index	$\sqrt{N}$	800-2000	0.3-0.6	0.3-1
Hierarchic Block Index (ISAM)	$1.24 \log_2 N$	200-800	0.2-0.3	0.3-1
Identifier Hashing	$N/\text{buckets}/2$	5-15	0.1-0.2	1-10

FIGURE 8.1: A Prescriptive Taxonomy for Record Access by Severance and Carlis

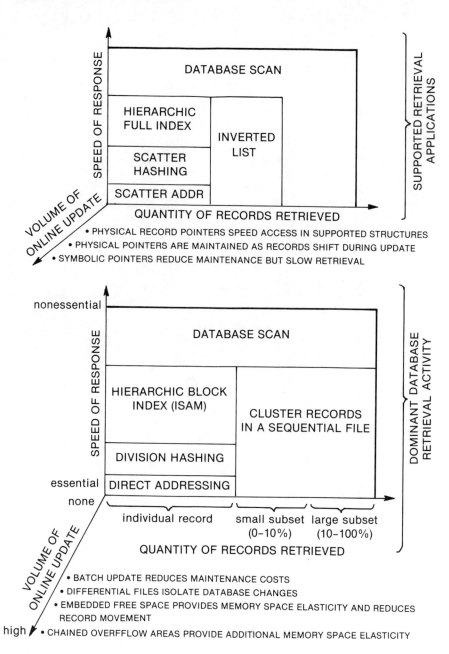

response, volume of on-line updates, and quantity of records retrieved (represented in Figure 8.1). The diagrams are specialized for primary or dominant data base activity (the bottom), and secondary applications (the upper diagram). The lower diagram prescribes the methods by which records are physically positioned in storage; the upper diagram prescribes techniques for accessing these records.

Optimizing Data Base Reorganization Points

As data and applications migrate over time, structural inefficiencies typically develop, causing increased data access and maintenance costs. Reorganizing the data base appropriately solves this problem, but the incremental cost associated with doing so forces a tradeoff between operational cost and reorganization cost, to achieve a minimum total cost. Shneiderman [17] has developed a tool, which considers these factors, for determining the best reorganization points.

Shneiderman's formulation of the case of reorganization with random deterioration of the search cost employs the following variables:

$C =$ excess search cost
$t =$ time interval between reorganizations
$T =$ total time
$\gamma_i =$ search cost during the ith interval
$N =$ number of reorganizations (T/t)
$R_i =$ reorganization cost during the ith interval

The cost density function in the ith interval is assumed to be a random variable $\gamma_i(t)$ with the distribution function

$$P(C|t) = \text{prob}\{\gamma_i(t)-C\}$$

It was recognized that there are two possible reorganization strategies: reorganization at fixed time intervals and reorganization when the search cost density has deteriorated to a given level (c). The fixed interval discipline has obvious operational advantages in terms of simplicity; but the question remains: Under what circumstances does each work best? The equations presented borrow heavily from the analysis of Eisen and Leibowitz [33].

For Discipline 1, the reorganization at fixed time intervals, the total cost of operating the system is

$$C(T) = \sum_{i=1}^{N} [\int_0^t \gamma_i(t')dt' + R_i(\gamma_i(t), t)]$$

The expected goal is to minimize total cost over time T with reorganization intervals of length t.

$$E[C(T)|t] = \sum_{i=1}^{N} [\int_0^t E[\gamma_i(t')]dt' + E[R_i(\gamma_i(t), t)]]$$

Two assumptions are then made: the cost density function is the same for each interval $\gamma_i(t) = \gamma(t)| i = 1 \ldots, N$, and the cost of reorganization is the same in each interval $R_i(\gamma_i(t), t) = R(\gamma(t), t)| i = 1 \ldots, N$; therefore,

$$E[C(T)|t] = T/t[\int_0^\infty E[\gamma(t')]dt' + E[R(\gamma(t), t)]]$$

$$\text{where } E[\gamma(t)] = \int_0^\infty C(dP(C|t)/dC)dC$$

$$E[R(\gamma(t), t)] = \int_0^\infty R(C, t)(dP(C|t)/dC)dC$$

The average cost rate for reorganization is minimal in this case, when $t = tm$ is selected to achieve the lowest value

$$[C(t)] = (E[C(t)|t]/T)$$

Discipline 2, for reorganization when search cost density has deteriorated to an arbitrary level C, assumes an average cost rate for reorganization at fixed density

$$[C(c)] = \lim_{T \to \infty} (E[C(T)|c]/T)$$

and the operating cost accumulated through time as

$$A(t) = \int_0^t \gamma(t')dt'$$

Eisen and Leibowitz have shown that

$$[C(c)] = (E[A|c] + E[R(c, t)|c])/E[t|c])$$

where $E[t|c]$, $E[A|c]$ and $E[R(c, t)|c]$ are the expected values of t, $A(t)$, and $R(c, t)$ when the cost density reaches the value c.

With a fixed cost density, the average cost ratio is minimized when $c = cm$ in the previous equation.

Shneiderman has shown that reorganization Discipline 2, involving the deterioration threshold c, results in lower total operating costs or is, at worst, equal to Discipline 1.

SUMMARY OF PSD TECHNIQUES

This chapter reviewed the literature relating to physical support definition. Three techniques were chosen and presented in detail. The first, by Hoffer [5], was offered as an effective solution technique for physical record design. The second, by Severance and Carlis [23], is a heuristic for selecting record access paths. Finally, an optimization model for data base reorganization points by Shneiderman [17] was presented. Together, these techniques solve some of the important physical data base design problems.

REFERENCES

1. M. E. Senko, V. Y. Lum and P. J. Owens, "A File Organization Evaluation Model (FOREM)," *Information Process-68* (1968): C19–C28.

2. Jair M. Babad, "A Record and File Partitioning Model," *Communications of the ACM* 20 (1977) 1: 22–31.

3. P. Dearnly, "A Model of a Self-Organizing Data Management System," *The Computer Journal* 17 (1974) 1: 13–16.

4. Mark J. Eisner and Dennis G. Severance, "Mathematical Techniques for Efficient Record Segmentation in Large Shared Databases," *Journal of the Association for Computing Machinery* 23 (1976) 4: 619–25.

5. Jeffrey A. Hoffer, "A Clustering Approach to the Generation of Subfiles for the Design of a Computer Data Base" (Ph.D. dissertation, Cornell University, 1975).

6. IBM, "Time Automated Grid System (TAG): Sales and System Guide," White Plains, N.Y.: International Business Machines, Technical Publication GY20-0358-1, 2nd ed. (May 1971).

7. James B. Rothnie and Tomas Lozano, "Attribute Based File Organization in a Paged Memory Environment," *Communications of the ACM* 17 (1974) 2: 63–69.

8. Mario Schkolnick, "A Clustering Algorithm for Hierarchical Structures," *ACM Transactions on Database Systems* 2 (March 1977) 1: 27–44.

9. Frank H. Benner, "On Designing Generalized File Records for Management Information Systems," *AFIPS, Fall Joint Computer Conference* 31 (1967): 291–304.

10. Y. Milman, "An Approach to Optional Design of Storage Parameters in Databases," *Communications of the ACM* 20 (1977) 5: 347–50.

11. D. G. Severance and A. G. Merten, "Performance Evaluation of File Organizations Through Modeling," *Proceedings of the 27th National Conference, ACM* (1972): 1061–72.

12. J. A. van der Pool, "Optimal Storage Allocation for a File in Steady State," *IBM Journal of Research and Development* 17 (1973) 1: 27–38.

13. _____ "Optimum Storage Allocation for Initial Loading of a File," *IBM Journal of Research and Development* 16 (1972) 6: 579–86.

14. Alfonso F. Cardenas, "Evaluation and Selection of File Organization—A Model and System," *Communications of the ACM* 16 (1973) 9: 540–48.

15. K. M. Chandy and C. V. Ramamoorthy, "Optimization of Information Storage Systems," *Information and Control* 13 (1968) 6: 509–26.

16. Philip Clapson, "Improving the Access Time for Random Access Files," *Communications of the ACM* 20 (1977) 3: 127–35.

17. Ben Shneiderman, "Optimum Data Base Reorganization Points," *Communications of the ACM* 16 (1973) 6: 362–65.

18. William G. Tuel, Jr., "Optimum Reorganization Points for Linearly Growing Files," *ACM Transactions on Database Systems* 3 (March 1978) 1: 32–40.

19. S. B. Yao, K. S. Das and T. J. Teorey, "A Dynamic Database Reorganization Algorithm," *ACM Transactions on Database Systems* 1 (June 1976) 2: 159–74.

20. Wesley W. Chu, "Optimal File Allocation in a Multiple Computer System," *IEEE Transactions on Computers* C-18 (1970) 19: 885–89.

21. J. A. van der Pool, "Optimum Storage Allocation for a File with Open Addressing," *IBM Journal of Research and Development* 17 (1973) 2: 106–14.

22. David K. Chow, "New Balanced-File Organization Schemes," *Information and Control* 15 (1976): 377–96.

23. D. G. Severance and J. V. Carlis, "A Practical Approach to Selecting Record Access Paths," *Computing Surveys* 9 (1977) 4: 259–72.

24. Burton H. Bloom, "Some Techniques and Trade-Offs Affecting Large Data Base Retrieval Times," *Proceedings of the 24th National Conference ACM* (1969): 83–95.

25. A. J. Collmeyer and J. E. Shemer, "Analysis of Retrieval Performance for Selected File Organization Techniques," *AFIPS, Fall Joint Computer Conference* 37 (1970): 201–10.

26. Kenneth F. Siler, "A Stochastic Evaluation Model for Data Base Organizations in Data Retrieval Systems," *Communications of the ACM* 19 (1976) 2: 84–95.

27. Alfonso F. Cardenas, "Analysis and Performance of Inverted Data Base Structure," *Communications of the ACM* 18 (1975) 5: 253–63.

28. V. Y. Lum, "Multi-Attribute Retrieval with Combined Indexes," *Communications of the ACM* 13 (1970) 11: 660–65.

29. V. Y. Lum, H. Ling and M. E. Senko, "Analysis of a Complex Data Management Access Method by Simulation Modeling," *AFIPS, Fall Joint Computer Conference* 37 (1970): 211–22.

30. M. E. Senko, H. Ling, V. Y. Lum, H. R. Meadow, M. R. Bryman, R. J. Drake and B. C. Meyer, *File Design Handbook* (Contract AF 30602-69-C-0100) (Submitted to Rome Air Development Center, Air Force Systems Command, Griffiss Air Force Base, New York, by IBM, San Jose Research Laboratory, San Jose, California, and Federal Systems Division, Gaithersburg, Maryland, November 1967).

31. W. L. Maxwell and D. G. Severance, "Comparison of Alternatives for the Representation of Data Item Values in an Information System," *Data Base* 5 (1973) 2, 3, 4: 121–39.

32. V. Y. Lum, P. S. T. Yuem and M. Dodd, "Key-to-Address Transform Techniques: A Fundamental Performance Study on Large Existing Formatted Files," *Communications of the ACM* 14 (1971) 4: 228–39.

33. M. Eisen and M. Leibowitz, "Replacement of Randomly Deteriorating Equipment," *Management Science* 9 (January 1963): 263–76.

34. W. T. McCormick, Jr., P. J. Schweitzer, Jr., and T. W. White, "Problem Decomposition and Data Reorganization by a Clustering Technique," *Operations Research* 20 (September-October 1972) 5: 993–1009.

35. J. D. McKeen, *Search Mechanism Analysis Routine (SMAR): System Documentation* (St. Paul: University of Minnesota, 1977).

36. E. D. Knuth, *The Art of Computer Programming: Searching and Sorting*, vol. 3 (Reading, Mass.: Addison-Wesley, 1973), p. 722.

37. J. Martin, *Computer Data-Base Organization* (Englewood Cliffs, N.J.: Prentice-Hall, 1975), p. 588.

38. D. G. Severance, "Identifier Search Mechanisms: A Survey and Generalized Model," *Computing Surveys* 6 (September 1974) 3: 175–94.

PART III

DATA BASE ADMINISTRATION

INTRODUCTION

The data base administration activity is clearly important to individual users, data processing staff, and the user organization. As such, it is specialized in a manner to serve each of these groups. The succeeding chapters will be organized according to this specialization: User-DBA interface, Programmer-DBA interface, and DBA-DBMS(data base management system) interface. In addition, a chapter will be devoted to the organizational alternatives of the DBA activity.

The DBA has received some attention in the literature. Two major works have been provided, by CODASYL [1] and GUIDE-SHARE [2], that define the informational requirements of the activity. To be sure, there have been other papers [3,4], but these tend to be quite specialized and/or deal with topics no longer relevant to a broad segment of DBAs. Along with the changes occuring in DBMS, the DBA activity has been forced to adapt; and a number of trends can be cited, based on a survey of DBAs.*

    1. The DBA's orientation has shown tendencies toward changing from that of a technical to a more managerial role as the day-to-day technical problems of such complex systems stabilize.

    2. Although, initially, the trend was toward centralizing the activity, it was quickly found that a single individual could not handle it effectively; therefore, the DBA activity is now frequently being executed by a staff of specialists.

    3. There is some indication that the activity may be specialized according to corporate functional lines to better serve these user groups.

Bearing in mind the potential changes in the DBA activity, the following chapters will discuss the major areas of interest.

REFERENCES

1. CODASYL Systems Committee, *Feature analysis of Generalized Data Base Management Systems: April '71 Report* (New York: Association for Computing Machinery, 1971).

---

*This survey involved in-depth interviews with a group of geographically distributed DBAs who were asked, among other things, to discuss their most important problems.

2. GUIDE-SHARE Data Base Requirements Group, *Data Base Management System Requirements* November 11, 1970.

3. Jean-Paul DeBlasis and Thomas H. Johnson, "Data Base Administration—Classical Pattern, Some Experiences and Trends," *Proceedings of the National Computer Conference* (1977): 1–7.

4. Jean-Paul DeBlasis and Thomas H. Johnson, "Review of Data Base Administrators Functions from a Survey," *Proceedings of SIGMOD International Conference on Management of Data, ACM*(1978): 101–9.

9

THE USER-DBA INTERFACE

INTRODUCTION

The user-DBA interface consists of those informational transfers necessary for the user to define desired system requirements and for the DBA to explain or justify processing constraints. That is to say, a dialogue is necessary. The dialogue is couched in the system's analysis activity; therefore, the best way to understand the special features and problems of the user-DBA interface is to consider systems analysis in a data base environment.

Chapter 6, in part, covered material relevant to the systems analysis activity. Chapter 9, instead of presenting cost-effective techniques for purposes of analysis, will describe the nature of the user-DBA relationship and issues relating to its management.

A TAXONOMY OF THE USER-DBA INTERFACE

The user-DBA interface involves three characteristic types of activities, all of which are peculiar to operational environments with a DBMS:

Training in data base concepts:
Loss of physical possession of user-data.

    User/provider of data may be different.
    Possibility of greater interconnectedness.
Mediate conflicting user demands:
    Response time.
    Storage space and form.
    Differential security of shared data.
    Differential integrity of shared data.
    User/provider of data may be different.
Assistance with additional technical capabilities:
    Real-time availability.
    Unstructured query.

Each of these activities is critical to the success of the supported information processing systems (IPS). The concepts of data base technology are sufficiently different from application-specific methods; to exploit the potential advantages the user almost must be retrained. In addition, the many potential advantages that accrue from system integration require a different user-interaction discipline, often resulting in slight local compromises, so global information advantages can be enjoyed. Finally, DBMS technology often brings with it, or is often associated with, capabilities also possible with conventional application-specific methods. The important issues involved in each of these activities will be discussed in the following sections.

Training in Data Base Concepts

There are a number of concepts characteristic of data base systems. One of the most difficult for users to adapt to is that they might not have physical possession of application data. The historical precedent is for users to have systems that are written specifically for them and that process files dedicated to those systems. This has resulted in users, at least, having the concept of a specific file such as a tape or disk that is theirs, and that could, if needed, be retrieved by them for purposes of safety. Obviously, in practice this may be quite impractical. With data base systems, however, users share data, and thereby relinquish the right, if not the ability, to physically possess "their" data. In a recent survey of DBAs by the author, the following statements were made by administrators when asked what was the most difficult problem faced by the DBA: "Taking away the possession of user data and direct control over it"; "Establishing credibility and modifying the concept of 'own data'"; and "Users giving up the concept of 'own data.'"

Users must understand that part of the price of data base systems capability is giving up possession of their data. Any comfort they enjoyed with the notion of possible physical possession is not likely to be warranted.

Perhaps the most striking characteristic of DBMS technology is that the user of information and the provider of the requisite data are often not the same, and may not even be in the same functional area. The effect of this is that the general knowledge of a single-source user/provider cannot be assumed to exist. For example, the provider of certain data may make the decision to change collection methods, which may result in a higher error rate in that data. The user, if the same person, is naturally aware of this change and the likely effects on related systems. However, if the user is in another department there must be an explicit communication to this effect, if not a joint decision, concerning the desirability of such a change. The number of possible areas for confusion because of the user and provider being different persons are too numerous to mention; however, the following list contains some characteristics of data requiring explicit definition to avoid confusion:

1. data name, synonyms and meanings
2. degree of aggregation
3. currency, when updated
4. accuracy, precision
5. security, retention
6. privacy or need to know, shareability
7. source
8. unit of measure

The final conceptual area for user training relates to the potential complexity of relationships (interconnectedness) among data available using a DBMS. The ability to handle more logical complexity is derived from three characteristics of DBMSs:

1. The user has access to a much greater variety of data; hence, greater complexity results if it is used;
2. Frequently, advanced technologies such as real-time data availability and an unstructured query facility, allow the user to support inherently complex applications that otherwise might not be practical; and
3. Users progress through a life cycle, one of the latter steps of which is the use of DBMS technology to support the processing required of the seasoned computer user and functional managers.

To be sure, there are other concepts of data base deserving discussion; nevertheless, these will suffice here. The major point suggested here is that users must be indoctrinated. In fact, a continual dialogue must exist between the user and the DBA, for without it the only change that DBMS will bring is increased costs.

Mediate Conflicting User Demands

The support system for all user requests is necessarily limited in a variety of ways, and, as was discussed in the previous section, the data is highly integrated, leading to dependent performance of system support. The following paragraphs will explore some of the potential interdependencies that necessitate mediating conflicting user demands.

Although from a performance point of view it is obvious that mutiple on-line users of a data base will have an effect on one another's response time, there is another performance effect that originates from data base technology. One might recall, from Chapter 2, the data control philosophy that attempts to reduce the redundancy of data from the traditional application-specific method and thereby enhance data security and integrity. Along with this possible reduction of redundancy, however, is the problem of concurrently supporting the data needs of several users. As long as both, or all, users want only to read the data, there is no problem. However, if one desires to update a datum while another reads it, what discipline should be involved? The problem of coordinating concurrent updates is complex; therefore, the method used most frequently is that of lockout, whereby the first user to access a datum in a write mode effectively prevents all others from retrieving it until the lockout has been removed, thus delaying execution.

Storage space, too, must be shared by all users of the data base. Although this may have a variety of effects on performance, the one of primary importance is the form in which a given shared datum will exist. For example, one user may want packed decimal; another, pure binary code. Since the data will be stored in only one way, one user must transform the data prior to use. The DBA must decide who will transform data, based on measures of system performance efficiency. Related to this is the issue of storing data in its usable form or in a virtual form [1]. Virtual data, of course, must be derived from its component parts and is not just a simple transformation as in the previous example. For example, the average salary level of all employees in a firm might be relevant for planning purposes and can either be derived (that is, is virtual) or stored directly.

Data security may also be affected in a DBMS environment. According to the Association for Computing Machinery (ACM) [2], data security refers to the protection of data against accidental or intentional disclosure to unauthorized persons, unauthorized modification, or destruction. Although application-specific systems do not explicitly ignore security, their lack of centralized data control makes them particularly susceptible to breaches in security. In a data base system where many users depend on a single or limited set of data, security is critical regardless of how casually one user views responsibility for data. The solution for differential security of shared data is a difficult one and requires a combination of data policy and system-programmed enforcement. The following principles might serve as a basis for a firm's data policy:

1. The data creator is responsible for use determination; that is, who can use it and how (for example, read only, read/write, or write only). The data creator must also determine file retention and backup policies.

2. The need to know concept might be useful; only those who need access to particular data will be granted access to it; therefore, no unauthorized browsing.

3. Where a discrepancy exists between the security required for data and the inherent security of a process requesting access to it, can the data be used in some other form? For example, a program designed to print average salary information for each management level might better be given virtual data for an average, rather than each employee's salary upon which to make the calculation. In some cases access may simply have to be denied.

4. Periodic or random checks for compliance with policies should be exercised.

5. In a few cases, security provisions are defined by law and must therefore be complied with according to the specified regulations.

Data integrity has been defined as existing when data does not differ from its source document and has not been accidentally or maliciously altered, disclosed, or destroyed. Related to data integrity is the concept of accuracy, which is a relative measure of how closely some attribute value represents the condition or state of an entity. Just as it is important, particularly in a DBMS environment, to control security, data integrity must also be monitored and controlled. Not only is data integrity required to insure proper management decision making but also to prevent unrecoverable errors from occurring. Undetected errors tend to migrate through a system and as this migration progresses it becomes more difficult to correct. Although several theories have been developed for error detection and for restart and recovery, it is still far from being a reliable process. It therefore behooves the DBA to establish and enforce standards promoting integrity and although many of these (such as checkpointing and structured programming) relate to the programmer-DBA interface, the effect of lack of control falls on the user. The user must therefore specify, with the assistance of the DBA, the appropriate level of integrity and recovery. These specifications must then be translated, although not always objectively, into policies and controls to insure their achievement during operation.

Finally, the user/provider may be either different people or different organizational units. With regard to the activity of mediating conflicting user demands, this results in a number of potential problems in addition to those mentioned in the section on user training. As mentioned previously, there may be problems regarding integrity, security, accuracy, use, and meaning of the shared data. This is usually best resolved by assigning responsibility for each datum to some organizational unit that will define rules for its use. It is advisable to have some exception mechanism in the event of an impasse; for example, an information policy steering committee. Perhaps the toughest problem facing the DBA in this category results from the situation in which one organizational unit requires data that originates in, but is not useful to, some other unit. If the collection and maintenance effort attributable to this item is trivial, a problem may not exist; if the effort is major, who incurs the cost? Again, the information policy steering committee may be called upon for a resolution.

The surfacing of many subtle problems is not surprising when the simplicity of functionally independent, application-specific systems is dropped in favor of the data base approach. All of the undefined situations and vagaries that exist could be handled reasonably well because the users were providers of the data. With the data base approach this may no longer be the case, and the only solution is to explicitly define all of the user/provider knowledge which previously permitted the system to operate smoothly.

Assistance with Additional Technical Capabilities

There are, in general, two advanced technologies associated with the DBMS environment: real-time availability of data and unstructured query. As manager of the information resource, the DBA may be called upon to assist the user with these capabilities; for by doing so the advantages of data base technology can be more fully exploited. Real-time availability of data is a relatively new concept to management—at least to the extent provided by current systems. Certainly, real-time access to very large files was never practical in manual systems, and, although practical and useful in many third-generation systems, it wasn't until DBMS technology evolved that it became accepted as a "normal" procedure. The user, then, must be made aware of its capability and must consider this operational mode as an alternative, if not a necessity, for advanced decision-support systems. It is difficult to imagine many systems (for example, order entry, and reservations) in other than real time.

The second technical capability, unstructured query, is a very recent development in computer languages although, in a sense, managers have been accustomed to this type of query (but only through their service personnel). Now it is available and quite effective through a computer terminal. The types of query facilities available are too numerous to mention (a few examples were discussed in Chapter 4). Users will need assistance in finding applications for and in using this facility.

SUMMARY OF THE USER-DBA INTERFACE

This chapter has outlined a series of classic problems faced and activities performed by the DBA directly for the user. The taxonomy used for this purpose consisted of user training, mediating conflicting user requirements, and assistance with advanced technologies associated with data base systems. It was found that the integration of user applications and data results in a wide variety of subtle problems for the DBA, but that they can be managed or solved directly.

REFERENCES

1. J. J. Folinus, S. E. Madnick, and H. B. Schutzman, "Virtual Information in Data Base Systems," *FDT* 6 (1974) 2: 1-15.

2. ACM Ombudsman Committee on Privacy, *Privacy, Security, and the Information Processing Industry* (New York: Association for Computing Machinery, 1976).

10

THE PROGRAMMER-DBA INTERFACE

INTRODUCTION

The programmer-DBA interface is very important for the satisfaction of user requests and the efficient operation of data processing. Unlike the user-DBA interface, the types of information transfers are much more well defined and occur at more predictable times. The purpose of this chapter is to describe a wide range of communication between the application programmer and the DBA, and to discuss a number of important, related issues. The next section will present a taxonomy of the interface, followed by a series of subsections discussing each major category of data transferred at the interface.

A TAXONOMY OF THE PROGRAMMER-DBA INTERFACE

The taxonomy of the dialogue between the application programmer and the DBA contained below consists of three major categories, the first involving the complete user statement of system requirements for the proposed system or change of an existing one, the second the system support constraints that restrict the range of feasible programmed alternatives to the application programmer because of such things as hardware/software limitations and policies, and the third the review by the

DBA of the programmed system to insure that the user requirements have been, in some sense, met (this is primarily the responsibility of the systems analyst and designer) and none of the restrictions violated. If the proposed system has successfully passed all of the review processes, it then becomes a member of the production system—but not before.

1. Application System Requirements (provided by the user through the DBA to the programmer):
Functions.
Data, including security, integrity, and privacy restrictions.
2. System Support Constraints (provided by the DBA to the programmer):
Subschema definition.
Required security, integrity, and privacy controls.
Hardware/software restrictions.
3. Programmed Application System:
Proposed programs.
Test plan and results.
Documentation package.

Application System Requirements

Part of the information necessary for the application programmer to create an operational system is a clear, concise statement of the application system requirements relating to functions and data. A number of techniques have already been discussed (see Chapter 6) that provide a vehicle for functional specification; these will not be repeated here. They do not, however, provide much assistance in specifying data requirements, except determining required attributes and their format. Therefore, the application programmer must decide or be told (the latter is obviously preferable) what security, integrity, and privacy procedures are required by the user (there may be additional restrictions imposed but that are not user-specified; these will be documented later).

The user may have specified a number of security and integrity restrictions that necessitate edit controls. Although these are well covered in the literature [1-9], essentially they consist of the following types:

1. Field composition test. Determine whether characters of the correct type are present in a field (for example, alphanumeric, numeric, and non-zero).
2. Valid character test. Whenever a limited set of characters is allowed in a field this method is used; may, for example, check for letters A through N in a given field.
3. Sign test. Validate the sign of a field whose sign is known and fixed.

4. Field size test. Insures that a field of an assumed width is, in fact, that wide.

5. Validation of check digits. Can detect substitution or transpositions of numeric values.

6. Presence of data. Determine whether all data required for some system event is present.

7. Authorization test. Appropriate for validating source of data. May be accomplished by checking for the presence of some "secret" value or coded "signature."

8. Transaction-type test. Where transactions of certain specified types occur, determines whether each is among that set.

9. Consistency test. Looks at a combination of fields and allowable dependent values.

10. Limit of reasonableness. Determines whether a received value is within a specified range.

11. Sequence check. If a sequence of transactions, for example, is important and identified, it is scanned to determine compliance with the assumed sequence.

It is the responsibility of the systems analyst to elicit the need for these controls and determine how they might be used singly or in comparison with one another to insure the security and integrity of the data base. To be sure, controls to enhance security and integrity are not limited to these: policies for computer operation and other matters may be used as well, but the application program controls typically consist of these methods.

Privacy of data also must be maintained in some situations, particularly for those systems handling personal information. Although there is no federal law relating to data use in the private sector (the Federal Privacy Act of 1974 applies only to government agencies),there is one pending (H. R. 1984) for which consideration was begun in 1975. In addition, there are a number of state, local, and foreign laws in existence. Unfortunately for the DBA, the whole area of privacy is changing rapidly as more states begin to initiate their own legislation. This will have significant effects on systems design. Consider the possibility of restricting the use of social security numbers as a standard identifying code for personnel. It is both impractical and beyond the scope of this book to outline the privacy issues. The interested reader is referred to ACM [10], Hoffman [11], Baruch [12], Bushkin [13], and Martin [14].

System Support Constraints

The DBA, as the responsibility center for a firm's information resource, must impose constraints on the application programmer and the systems design staff in three major categories: subschema definitions or the program's view of the data base; system-wide security, integrity, and privacy controls; and hardware/software restrictions.

The imposition of a single data authority in the DBA [15] has removed from programmers the authority to define their own data and still maintain efficient structures for the entire user community. This necessitates that the DBA be responsible for and issue each program's data definition, the subschema.

Chapter 4 presented a series of data definition models that may well serve to demonstrate the type of information passed from the DBA to the application programmer. For example, a construction can be made of the data definitions required for the logical structure in Figure 10.1:

FIGURE 10.1:   A Student-Class Data Base

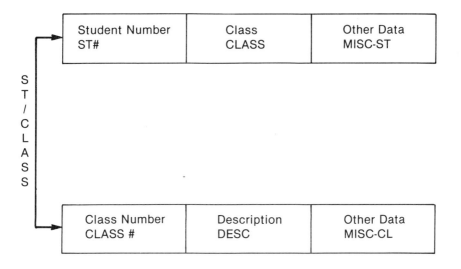

In this example are two record types: a student record containing a student number (ST#), class (CLASS), and various detail items (MISC-ST), and a class record containing class number (CLASS #), class description (DESC), and other data (MISC-CL). For each student there may be one or more student records, each of which is described by a corresponding class record, the relationship being denoted by ST/CLASS. The ST/CLASS relationship is implemented quite simply by storing the value (or its equivalent)

of the class number of the class record in each class field of the student record.

Two examples of data definition will be presented. One is a CODASYL subschema defined in the subschema DDL (Data Definition Language) contained in Figure 10.2, the second is written in IBM's DL/I (Figure 10.3). Although the first example contains only a few of the possible statements available to CODASYL DDL users, it does give a limited but useful picture of the language. The first statement specifies a logical name associated with the schema or data base. The area specification is CODASYL's method of providing a fine-tuning aid by which the data base designer may name and specify a physical location wherein the data base will exist. Although many of these may be used, perhaps one or more per record type, for our purposes only one is deemed appropriate. The record for the student file is named STUDENT and to enhance security and privacy a privacy procedure named STUDENT is to be invoked any time a record is accessed. The contents of the procedure would then be defined as with any other program. The record structure is specified using the data structure facilities of the COBOL language. Correspondingly, the record contents for the class data are also defined. CODASYL uses sets as a logical building block for data structures; these are named, and, in this case, the set of class records is called CLASSES. The owner record of the set (that is, the record through which access is gained) is the student record, and the set named CLASSES consists of all occurrences of the record CLASS. The set is to be permanently (as opposed to temporarily) maintained in ascending sequence, based on the field CLASS#, and no duplicates are allowed (identical values for CLASS #).

FIGURE 10.2: Example of CODASYL Subschema DDL

```
SCHEMA NAME IS ST-CLASS-DATA
AREA NAME IS CLASS-DATA
RECORD NAME IS STUDENT
PRIVACY LOCK IS STUDENT
      01 ST#          PIC "9(9)"
      01 CLASS        PIC "9(4)"
      01 MISC-ST      PIC "9(10)"
RECORD NAME IS CLASS
      01 CLASS #      PIC "9(4)"
      01 DESC         PIC "X(25)"
      01 MISC-CL      PIC "9(10)"
SET NAME IS CLASSES; ORDER IS PERMANENT
      OWNER IS STUDENT
      MEMBER IS CLASS; ASCENDING KEY IS
          CLASS #; DUPLICATES NOT ALLOWED
```

FIGURE 10.3:   Example of DL/I's "Subschema" DDL

```
DBD       NAME = ST-CLASS-DATA, ACCESS = HDAM, . . . . .
DATASET DD1 = SCHDAM,DEVICE = 3330,BLOCK = . . . .
SEGM      NAME = STUDENT,BYTES = 23,FREQ = 1000
FIELD     NAME = (ST#,SEQ,U)BYTES = 9,START = 1,TYPE = P
FIELD     NAME = CLASS,BYTES = 4,START = 10,TYPE = P
FIELD     NAME = MISC-ST,BYTES = 10,START = 14,TYPE = C
SEGM      NAME = CLASS,BYTES = 39,FREQ = 100,PARENT = STUDENT
FIELD     NAME = (CLASS#,SEQ,U),BYTES = 4,START = 1,TYPE = P
FIELD     NAME = DESC,BYTES = 25,START = 5,TYPE = P
FIELD     NAME = MISC-CL,BYTES = 10,START = 30,TYPE = C
DBDGEN
```

Note that the subschema DDL is not pure in the sense of logical and physical references. Nevertheless, CODASYL has succeeded in defining a DDL that is relatively free of physical details and is of little direct concern to the application programmer. The difference is best demonstrated through the same example definded in IBM's DL/I, as shown in Figure 10.3.

DL/I begins with a data base definition (DBD) statement that includes the name, access method to be used, and a number of other physical parameters of the ST-CLASS-DATA data base. The data base, in turn, consists of a single data set (physical file) with two physical record types (SEGM's). The data set also must be defined in terms of a variety of parameters, including the device types and blocking size. Each of the physical records or segments must have a logical name, the number of characters (bytes) contained, the number of occurrences of that record type, and, in the case of the segment CLASS, the parent (owner) segment. Each field is defined, indicating the total number of characters, the beginning point of the first character and the type of character used to represent the value, and whether it functions as a key.

It is quite obvious that DL/I places a much heavier physical specification burden on the DBA than does CODASYL's subschema DDL. The type of information provided in these specifications can only be given by the DBA for several reasons: only the DBA has the user-wide systems viewpoint to choose the required data base structures that force compromises on individual users but offer some degree of system optimality; for security reasons, only the DBA should have access to this information; and the application programmer should not be expected to be expert enough to adequately define these parameters.

The DBA's concern for the constraints on system support also include security, integrity, and privacy issues. Although essentially the same techniques are employed as mentioned in the previous section, the goal is quite different. Although security, integrity, and privacy restrictions are placed at the application level, these are used primarily to protect the application system. System support's overriding concern, however, is more general: to protect the user or application community from unfriendly or unsocial program behavior or user behavior. It is, therefore, neither obvious nor particularly important that a given control procedure enhances a given application—just global system support. A checkpoint procedure prevents an application program from having to be completely rerun in a variety of situations, as well as from disrupting all other user tasks during the rerun.

Hardware and software restrictions also may be imposed by the DBA to enhance security, integrity, or privacy, or simply to insure operational efficiency. Undoubtedly, operational efficiency as measured by such as turn-around or response time can have an important effect on user satisfaction and, therefore, the success of the IPS. The DBA must then measure these parameters and control the allocation of hardware and software resources to satisfy user requirements through the application programmer.

Programmed Application System

In the first two sections of the taxonomy of the programmer-DBA interface, communications from the DBA to the programmer were dominant, although in reality a dialogue may have been necessary. The final section addresses those communications that are typically necessary during the final system development steps and exist primarily to permit the DBA to confirm that the various specifications and constraints set in the previous two sections have been observed and met.

The proposed programs to be used to service a user's request must be reviewed by the DBA prior to being turned over for production. Although the subschema is a vehicle for insuring compliance with some of the programming standards and operational constraints (for example, read-only access and password protection), others must be confirmed through a check of the procedures themselves. Examples of these are the inclusion of checkpoints, or rollback procedures, and edit checks. The author [16] has found that the appropriate type of attribute use also may be important and, therefore, should be monitored. Consider the case in which attributes are accessed from the data base but never used. Not only does this occur surprisingly often, it also biases data base design [17] and causes operational inefficiency (not to mention potential security and integrity problems). In addition to general procedural details of the proposed application programs, the programming methodology (language, structure, etc.) should be checked and, particularly in a real-time environment, the efficiency of the code must be considered and adjusted if necessary.

The DBA is also responsible at least indirectly for the test plan of all operational systems accessing the data base. The test plan must, therefore, be explicit regarding how the test data is generated, how it insures that each branch within the program is properly executed, and whether any live system data is used. Although software reliability is beyond the scope of this discussion, any methods of this type that are employed should be defined and the results noted. In addition, a structured walkthrough may be a method of programmer-DBA review. Not only is this an advantage of advanced programming technology, it can be employed by the DBA for purposes of this activity.

Finally, the DBA is responsible for the full range of documentation relating to the data base. The data dictionary/directory (DD/D) system is used, in part, for this purpose and is maintained by the DBA. Although data definitions for the schemas and subschemas compose part of the DD/D descriptions of programs, systems and even source documents may also be included [18]. Since the DD/D is part of the DBMS, it will be discussed in detail in Chapter 11.

SUMMARY OF THE PROGRAMMER-DBA INTERFACE

This chapter has, in a sense, made an input/output analysis of the programmer-DBA interface. It has been shown that the application system requirements derived from the users, with the assistance of systems analysts, and translated into workable systems designs are passed through the DBA to the application programmer, along with other necessary information in the form of system support constraints (for example, subschema, edit checks, and hardware/software restrictions). The programmer returns with application programs, test results of trial runs, and a complete documentation package for review by the DBA prior to the system being approved for production.

REFERENCES

1. AICPA, "Computer Auditing Subcommittee's Auditing Advanced EDP Systems Task Force, Advanced EDP Systems and the Auditor's Concern," *Journal of Accountancy* (January 1975).

2. Barry R. Chaiken and William E. Perry, "ITF—A Promising Computer Audit Technique," *Journal of Accountancy* (February 1973).

3. M. M. Hammer and D. J. McLeod, "A Framework for Semantic Integrity," *Proceedings of the II International Conference on Software Engineering* (October 1976).

4. R. C. T. Lee, et al., "Application of Clustering to Estimate Missing Data and Improve Data Integrity," *Proceedings of the II International Conference on Software Engineering* (October 1976).

5. C. Machgeels, "A Procedural Language for Expressing Integrity Constraints in the Coexistence Model," *Proceedings of IFIP TC-2 Working Conference on Modeling in Data Base Management Systems* (January 1976).

6. M. R. Stonebreaker, *High Level Integrity Assurance in Relational Data Base Management Systems*, Technical Report ERL-M473 (Berkeley, Calif.: University of California–Berkeley, 1974).

7. M. R. Stonebreaker, "Implementation of Integrity Constraints and Views of Query Modification," *Proceedings of ACM-SIGMOD International Conference on Management of Data* (May 1975).

8. H. Weber, "A Semantic Model of Integrity Constraints in a Relational Data Base," *Proceedings of IFIP TC-2 Working Conference* (January 1976).

9. H. L. Weiss, "The Use of Audit Indication and Integrated Test Facility Techniques," *EDPACS* (July 1973).

10. ACM Los Angeles Chapter Ombudsman Committee on Privacy, *Privacy, Security, and the Information Processing Industry"* (New York: ACM, 1976).

11. Lance J. Hoffman, *Modern Methods for Computer Security and Privacy* (Englewood Cliffs, N.J.: Prentice-Hall, 1977).

12. Jordan Baruch, "The Economics of Providing Privacy," *NBS/MITRE* (1975): 82-89.

13. A. A. Bushkin and S. I. Schaen, *The Privacy Act of 1974: A Reference Manual for Compliance* (McLean, Va.: System Development Corp., 1976).

14. J. Martin, *Security, Accuracy, and Privacy in Computer Systems* (Englewood Cliffs, N.J.: Prentice-Hall, 1973).

15. E. H. Sibley, "The Development of Data-Base Technology," *Computing Surveys* 8 (March 1976) 1: 1-5.

16. Jon D. Clark, "An Attribute Access Probability Determination Procedure" (Ph.D. dissertation, Case Western Reserve University, 1977).

17. Jon D. Clark and J. A. Hoffer, "A Procedure for the Determination of Attribute Access Probabilities," *Proceedings of ACM-SIGMOD International Conference on Management of Data* (1978).

18. P. P. Uhrowczik, "Data Dictonary/Directories," *IBM Systems Journal* 4 (1973): 332-50.

11

THE DBA-DBMS INTERFACE

INTRODUCTION

The final system interface to be discussed in this section is that formed by the interaction between the DBA and the data base management system (DBMS). It is through this interface that the DBA sets policies and restrictions on data base use in a manner permitting a great deal of programmed controls, which is partly imposed through subschema definitions. In addition, it is this interface that provides an entry point for system documentation to be stored and managed by the data dictionary/directory (DD/D). The succeeding sections will develop and discuss a taxonomy of activity between the DBA and the DBMS.

A TAXONOMY OF THE DBA-DBMS INTERFACE

Any discussion of the DBA-DBMS interface must include the following four topics: performance monitoring; data base audit; system improvement; and the storage and maintenance of the data base's own information system, the DD/D. The first three—performance monitoring, data base audit, and system improvement—will each have a chapter dedicated in the next section; therefore, only the DBA's relationship with the DD/D will be discussed here.

A relatively large number of articles have appeared in the literature (for example, [1] through [8]) regarding DD/D and its potential as a management tool. In particular, Uhrowczik [9] has captured the most general and comprehensive use of this mechanism; and it will, therefore, serve as a model for use in this chapter. The taxonomy of the DBA-DBMS interface, implemented through the DD/D, is given in the following list and will be followed in the remaining sections of this chapter.

> 1. Content:
>   Data descriptions.
>   Process descriptions.
>   Other entity descriptions.
> 2. Operational Modes:
>   Active.
>   Passive.

This typology will be useful because it recognizes that data about data, processes, and other data processing entities (or meta-data) are of use to the DBA and the DBMS; and, furthermore, the DD/D may be employed either as an off-line (passive) or on-line (active) tool. The succeeding subsections will illustrate these potential uses and corresponding contents.

DD/D Content

Prior to discussing the potential uses of DD/D, the contents must be considered. In doing so, we may draw upon Uhrowczik [9] and characterize all application systems as consisting of a number of entities. These are presented in hierarchical form in Figure 11.1. Note the three classes of entity descriptions. Class 1 (data descriptions) consists of data and storage structure terms, and, although not defined identically with the terms presented in Chapter 3, they serve well to describe both the logical and physical characteristics of data. As is characteristic of terminology in this area, the distinction between logical and physical concepts is not always clear. Class 2 (process descriptions) is composed of process, job, and system definitions arranged in hierarchical form; these too, may be used effectively to define user applications. Class 3 consists of general entity descriptors for a wide range of functions; others are certainly possible.

Each of the entities may be described by a number of parameters. Table 11.1 contains a set of possible parameters and indicates their applicability to each of the entities. The DBA can fully describe application systems by using these entities and their description; in a sense, constructing a specialized bill of material for data processing applications, as shown in Figure 11.2. Although this is not intended to be a generally applicable figure, it does give an example of a possible logical structure.

FIGURE 11.1: Potential Entity Descriptions

Data Descriptions	Element (EL)	The smallest independent unit of data referenced by a process.
	Group (GR)	A grouping of logically related elements and/or groups. Typically this is the user's view of data, the logical record in COBOL.
	Physical Segment (PS)	The smallest unit of accessible data residing on secondary storage.
	Data Set (DS)	Sometimes called a physical file, this is a grouping of physical segments on secondary storage. In many cases a data set consists of two or more physical segment types.
	Data Base (DB)	One or more related data sets or data bases.
Process Descriptions	Process (PR)	A procedure that accomplishes a specific data processing task such as a job step or program.
	Job (JO)	A self-contained set of related processes that forms a unit in itself.
	System (SY)	A combination of jobs forming an entire application system.
	Transaction (TR)	A specific set of input data that triggers the execution of a specific process or job.
	Report (RE)	Information presented to a person. This may be in the form of a printed report or a display on a CRT.

(continued)

FIGURE 11.1: (Continued)

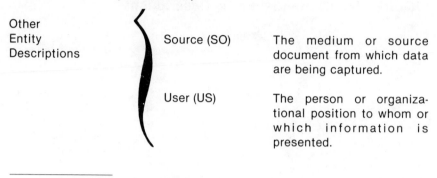

Other
Entity
Descriptions

Source (SO) — The medium or source document from which data are being captured.

User (US) — The person or organizational position to whom or which information is presented.

Note: These groupings of entities are the author's, not Uhrowzck's.

Although much of the information suggested in Table 11.1 is available, infrequently is it in machine-readable form. In addition, many inconsistencies and omissions may exist in this current documentation. This presents a serious problem to the DBA, and few techniques have been offered in the literature,* or in practice, that lend relief. From an implementation point of view it is well worth the effort to plan ahead and devote adequate resources to developing the DD/D.

DD/D Operational Modes

There are two extreme modes of DD/D operation: active and passive. The latter, referred to by Uhrowczik [9] as the "management use mode," is employed as a basic off-line tool for company management, the DBA, systems analysts, and application programmers for planning, controlling, and evaluating the data resource. As such, it depends on the enforcement of restrictions based on policies only. The other extreme is the active mode, referred to by Uhrowczik as the "computer use mode." It relies on the DD/D being in machine-readable form, and uses the computer to enforce compliance with various restrictions such as access authorization. The implementation of an active DD/D is one opportunity for data processing to apply its own technology to the solution of one of its own problems. Some examples appear in the following list and rely heavily on the entity descriptions advocated by Uhrowczik and the potential for programmed management assistance.

1. Assist in controlling undesirable redundancy by identifying synonyms.
2. Aid in the prevention of inconsistency through identifying homonyms.

---

*Although a number of the data base design aids discussed in Chapters 6, 7, and 8 serve as data collection methods, only Clark [10] has written specifically about the DD/D initialization problem.

TABLE 11.1: Entity Descriptors

Entity descriptions	Entities										
	EL	GR	PS	DS	DB	PR	JO	SY	TR	RE	SO
LABLE (Unique ID)	X	X	X	X	X	X	X	X	X	X	X
VERSION	X	X	X	X	X	X	X	X	X	X	X
STATUS (Proposed, concurred, approved, effective)	X	X	X	X	X	X	X	X	X	X	X
SPECIFICATION RESPONSIBILITY	X	X	X	X	X	X	X	X	X	X	X
CONTENT RESPONSIBILITY	X	X	X	X	X	X	X	X	X	X	X
LAST CHANGED DATE	X	X	X	X	X	X	X	X	X	X	X
TEXTUAL DESCRIPTION (Common name, meaning, purpose)	X	X	X	X	X	X	X	X	X	X	X
DESIGNATOR (A set of key words that best describes the meaning)	X	X	X	X	X	X	X	X	X	X	X
SYNONYM (Other DD/D entry with same meaning but different label)	X	X		X	X	X		X	X	X	X
* LENGTH (Characters)	X	X	X	X				X	X		
* MODE (Bit string, character string, packed decimal, simple floating point)	X					X					
* PRECISION (For numeric elements)	X										
* JUSTIFICATION (right, left)	X										
* PICTURE (For display purposes only)	X	X									
* EDIT RULES (Constant, range of values, edit mask, table)	X	X	X								
DERIVATION ALGORITHM (For calculated elements)	X										
* KEY	X	X									
* INDEX	X	X									

TABLE 11.1 (Continued)

Data Element									
UNIT (pounds, inches, dollars)	X								
*SEQUENCE (The sequential position that this item occupies in the membership)	X	X	X						
LANGUAGE SYNONYM (such as COBOL name)	X	X	X	X					
VOLUME (Number of data set or data base records)			X	X					
GROWTH FACTOR (Growth in the number of records in a given time period)			X	X					
ORGANIZATION (SAM, VSAM, HIDAM, etc.)			X	X					
SECURITY (Security code for read, update)	X	X	X	X			X		
DESTINATION								X	X
MEDIUM (Card, disk, tape, video)		X	X				X	X	X
SORT SEQUENCE (Name of elements/groups upon which the sequence is maintained)			X	X					
*UPDATE RULES (IMS use)		X		X					
*PROCESSING OPTIONS (IMS use)	X	X		X					
*PARENT (For IMS, who is the parent of the segment in this DB)		X	X						
*RELATION (For IMS, the 4 basic relationships; PP, LP, PCH, LCH)			X						
PROGRAMMING LANGUAGE					X	X			
PROGRAM TYPE (Batch, TP)					X	X			
MEMBERSHIP (Entities of which this item is a member or is being referenced by)	X	X	X	X	X	X	X	X	X

Source: Courtesy of International Business Machines Corporation.

FIGURE 11.2: Entity Relationships Described in a DD/D

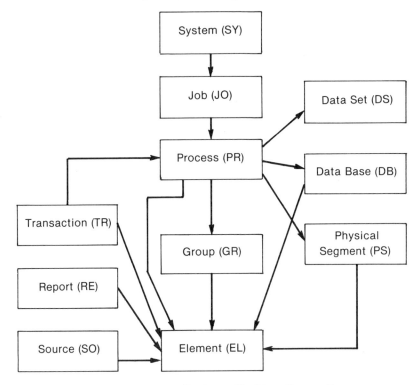

Source: Courtesy International Business Machines Corporation.

3. Reduce application systems development and implementation lead times and costs by insuring complete and accurate data description.

4. Provide a system for impact analysis capability for both maintenance and new system development, relying heavily on the directory function.

5. Enforce access restrictions and integrity procedures.

6. Identification and control of data and system responsibility.

7. Serve as a vehicle for the collection, storage, and analysis of data and system use statistics.

8. Provide control of system versions as applications migrate.

9. Force a standard format and methodology of documentation.

Table 11.2 suggests a variety of uses of the DD/D by user type. Not surprising is that the primary beneficiaries of its use are the DBA and the systems analyst. However, the DBMS can well employ the data definition capability for mapping subschemas into the schema. In addition, data

TABLE 11.2: Possible Users of DD/D Capabilities

APPLICATION SYSTEMS PLANNER	SPONTANEOUS USER	DP MANAGEMENT	DATA BASE ADMINISTRATOR	SYSTEMS ANALYST	PROGRAMMER	COMPILERS	DBMS	
x			x	x				A GENERALIZIED DEFINITION OF DATA
x	x		x	x				B REDUNDANT/INCONSISTENT DATA DETECTION
			x	x	x			C VERSION CONTROL
			x	x	x			D WHERE USED
x		x	x	x				E PLANNING INQUIRY
x	x	x	x	x	x			F COMMON DOCUMENTATION
				x	x			G GENERATION OF DATA DIVISION SOURCE DEFINITIONS
			x				x	H GENERATION OF MACRO PARAMETERS

MANAGEMENT USE   COMPUTER USE

Source: Courtesy International Business Machines Corporation.

processing management may find the DD/D useful for contingency planning [11], hardware/software selection decisions, and many typed ad hoc queries.

SUMMARY OF THE DBA-DBMS INTERFACE

Although it is recognized that the DBA-DBMS interface includes performance monitoring, audit, system improvement, and the storage and maintenance of the data base's own information system (the DD/D), Part IV of this book will have a chapter devoted to each of the first three areas of the interface; therefore, Chapter 11 addressed only the relationship between the DBA and the DD/D. A taxonomical approach was taken toward the DD/D, consisting of content (including descriptions of data processes and miscellaneous other entities) and the operational modes (both active and passive). A great deal of material was taken from an article by Uhrowczik [9], in which examples were drawn illustrating both content and use.

REFERENCES

1. John J. Cahill, "A Dictionary/Directory Method for Building a Common MIS Data Base," *Journal of Systems Management* 21 (November 1970) 11: 23-29.

2. P. J. H. King, "Systems Analysis Documentation: Computer Aided Data Dictionary Definition," *Computer Journal* 12 (1969): 6-9.

3. George N. Martin, "Data Dictionary/Directory System," *Journal of Systems Management* (December 1973): 12-19.

4. B. K. Plagman and G. P. Altshuler, "A Data Dictionary/Directory within the Context of an Integrated Corporate Data Base," *Proceedings of the AFIPS Fall Joint Computer Conference* 41 (1972) 11: 1133-40.

5. William B. Stevens, "The Concept of the Data Analysis and Control Catalogue for Management Information Systems," *Computers and Automation* (April 1968): 40-42.

6. William M. Taggart, Jr., *Developing an Organization's Information Inventory*, Working Paper 74-1 (Miami: Florida International University, 1974).

7. Eugene Wall, "Vocabulary Building and Control Techniques," *American Documentation* (April 1969): 161-64.

8. Michael L. Wearing, "Upgrade Documentation with a Data Dictionary," *Computer Decisions* (August 1973): 29-31.

9. P. P. Uhrowczik, "Data Dictionary/Directories," *IBM Systems Journal* 12 (1973) 4: 332-50.

10. J. D. Clark, "A Utility for the Generation of a Preliminary Data Dictionary Directory," *Proceedings of the 1978 Annual Conference, ACM* 78 (1978): 223-29.

11. Lord W. Kenniston, *The Data Center Disaster Consultant* (Wellesley, Mass.: Q.E.D. Information Science, 1977).

12

ORGANIZATIONAL ALTERNATIVES

INTRODUCTION

Prior to delineating several organizational structures for the DBA activity, additional descriptive material about the DBA's background is necessary. An in-depth survey of fourteen DBAs was performed by the author in Chicago, Cleveland, and New York. Those contacted were taken from user lists of a number of commercial DBMSs. Each responded in person to a set of standard questions, followed by an unstructured discussion of the activity. Table 12.1 is an industrial profile of the participants as they are comprised by the major sectors of the economy.

Table 12.2 depicts a variety of DBMS installations surveyed, with regard to the commercial system used, and includes IMS, ADABAS, IDMS, DMS, IDS, and a few independently designed and implemented systems. Although the sample size of respondents is small, the contents of Tables 12.1 and 12.2 indicate subjectively that it is not very biased.

Table 12.3 shows that exactly one-half of the DBMS installations had either a titled DBA or a data manager; the other half had no immediate plans for such a formal position.

Table 12.4 demonstrates an interesting fact: Three respondents considered the DBA activity to be primarily "managerial" in nature; eleven termed it "technical." One reason for this might be that the technology of data base is still relatively unsettled and, therefore, DBAs are faced with a

TABLE 12.1: Industrial Profile

Sector	Number of Respondents
Government	2
Service	6
Manufacturing	6

TABLE 12.2: DBMS Used

Types	Number of Respondents
Own	2
IMS	2
ADABAS	2
IDMS	3
DMS (6700 and 11)	4
IDS	2

Note: One participant used IMS and ADABAS; both were counted. This is not an unusual occurence, since the use to which each was put was inherently different. IMS was used for production jobs, ADABAS was employed for unstructured query applications.

TABLE 12.3: Titled DBA or Data Manager

Formal Title	Number of Respondents
Yes	7
No	7

TABLE 12.4: Role of DBA

Role	Number of Respondents
Managerial	3
Technical	11
No Response	1

Note: One participating firm had two DBAs—one technical, one managerial; both were counted.

large number of technical problems of a systems programming nature.

Another characteristic of the DBA population (Table 12.5) is the length of experience with DBMSs at the participating installations. Of the respondents, approximately 55% had two or more years of experience, and one individual had 11 years of experience. It is likely that a young and inexperienced DBA population would have a different class of problems than the older, more seasoned veterans, especially with respect to the mangerial/technical orientation previously discussed.

TABLE 12.5: Length of Time with DBMS

Length of Time	Number of Respondents
1 year or less	4
2 years or less (more than 1)	2
3 years or less (more than 2)	1
5 years or less (more than 3)	1
11 years or less (more than 5)	1
No Response	5

It was found (Table 12.6) that financial applications were typically the first implemented in the DBMS environment, followed by production and personnel (seven, three, and two respondents, respectively). Although this may not be particularly surprising, it is probably because of both the significance of financial applications and the relative ease with which they are implemented, as opposed to the inherent complexity of many production systems.

TABLE 12.6: First Application Implemented

Application	Number of Respondents
Financial	7
Production	3
Personnel	2
No Response	3

Note: One participant implemented both financial and personnel application initially; both were counted.

The DD/D concept [1] is quite popular, as is demonstrated in Table 12.7, and it was found that of 13 participants only three did not use, or intend to use, one. Six were currently working toward the implementation of a DD/D. Four respondents were using DD/Ds, three of which were of an active nature (that is, a certain amount of programmed decision making was triggered directly from the data contained in its structure). The remaining participant used this tool passively, or simply in a documentary mode.

TABLE 12.7: Use of DD/D

Use	Number of Respondents
Not used	3
Working toward	6
Have active system	3
Have passive system	1
No Response	1

Now that some of the characteristics of a sample of DBAs are known, as well as the operational environment within which they work, a number of organizational alternatives may be presented.

DBA ORGANIZATION

The organizational alternatives to be explored will be broken into the following classes: placement within the organization, organization of the activity among specialists, and job specifications for each of the specialists.*

Placement Within the Organization

The nature of the DBA activity dictates its location within a firm. Considering the independence necessary for the DBA to be able to evaluate and control all data use within an organization, the activity must be segregated from normal DP operations, in the same manner as the corporate comptroller's activity is, with regard to the various functions monitored by that position. In an attempt to satisfy this requirement, many organizations have their DBAs report to the director of information services. It is essential that the responsibility level be at least equal to that of the manager of DP; when information policies set by the DBA conflict with DPs operational tactics the final authority must be the director.

---

*See Martin [2] and Ross [3] for more material on these subjects.

Organization of the DBA Activity

In general, the DBA organization may be structured using functional or application specialization, as shown in Figures 12.1 and 12.2, respectively. In the first alternative, employing functional specialization of the various DBA tasks consists of four areas, each of which might be staffed by one or more individuals, depending on the volume of the administrative activity. The first specialist is the data definitional analyst, whose role is to interact with users and solve user-logical problems. The second, the data base design analyst, administers most of the technical data retrieval problems encountered. The third, data operations supervisor, handles the day-to-day, or frequently recurring, problems such as supervision of libraries and scheduling. Finally, a data security officer is included because of the importance of this activity.

FIGURE 12.1:   Functional Specialization of the DBA Activity

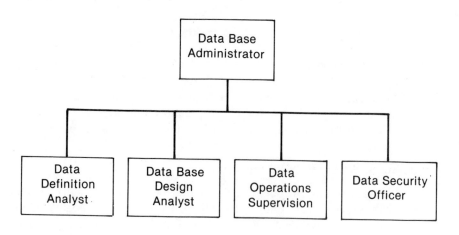

The second organizational alternative, application specialization, applies to the same activities of the data base design analyst, data operations

FIGURE 12.2: Application Specialization of the DBA Activity

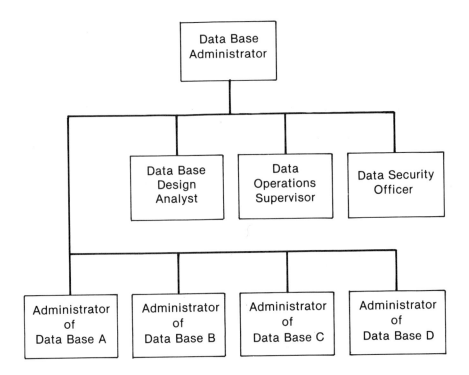

supervisor, and data security officer, but further specializes the data definition analyst activity to each functional area (for example, financial applications and plant operations). This provides more applications-dependent assistance to users. For organizations of moderate size, this assistance may entail only part-time activity; for large systems, full-time.

Each of these staff positions requires a particular type of background on the part of the individual in order that the job be performed competently. The data definition analyst need not be a computer scientist by training or a systems programmer by profession; logical skills are most important and they are, in general, well developed by those having a business degree in addition to moderate programming ability. The data base design analyst requires more in-depth technical training than does the data definition analyst. Some business information systems departments provide this, but it may be more commonly acquired in computer science departments and with practical experience. The data operations supervisor does not require quite the level of technical skills of the data base design analyst, but would benefit from supervisory and management skills either acquired in school or from practical experience. The data security officer requires a background similar to that of the data definition analyst. In addition, however, some sense of legal requirements would also prove useful, if not necessary, as increasingly restrictive privacy legislation is passed.

Job Specifications

The previous organizational alternatives of the DBS activity assumed certain job content for each of the specialized activities. The following list contains a brief outline of the general class of activities performed by each specialization. This outline is by no means exhaustive, but is only intended to serve as an example.

Data Definition Analyst:
Defines subschemas and schema.
Maintains documentation in DD/D.
Specifies data retention requirements.
Sets policies for validity, security, consistency, and accuracy.
Trains users in data base concepts.
Data Base Design Analyst:
Administers physical data base structure decisions and performance timing.
Makes hardware/software selection decisions, including access methods.
Design of restart and recovery system.
Monitors data base performance.
Selects security methods including encryption and description techniques.
Selects and administers privacy techniques.
Definition and implementing of concurrent updata avoidance methods.
Analysis of compaction techniques.
Advising of programmers.
Data Operations Supervisor:
Controls error detection and correction.
Supervises restart and recovery procedures.
Triggers reorganization of the data base.
Controls data retention and audit trail procedures.
Manages all libraries, including the DD/D.
Assists in scheduling data base applications.
Data Security Officer:
Assists in specification of all security/privacy procedures.
Investigates all security/privacy breaches.
Determines data access and use authorization.
Generates and modifies data locks and keys.
Performs security audit procedures.

SUMMARY OF THE DBA ACTIVITY

This chapter has covered the organizational aspects of the DBA activity. Beginning with the results of a descriptive survey of DBAs, their background, problems, and operational environment, two organizational alternatives were offered: functionally specialized and specialized according to applications. Although the general goal of this book is to cover the requirements of the entire DBA activity, various specialties (data definition, data base design, operation, and security) were discussed and staffing needs suggested in particular.

REFERENCES

1. P. P. Uhrowczik, "Data Dictionary/Directories," *IBM Systems Journal* 12 (1973) 4: 332–50.

2. James Martin, *Principles of Data-Base Management* (Englewood Cliffs, N.J.: Prentice-Hall, 1976), pp. 260–70.

3. Ronald G. Ross, *Data Base Systems: Design, Implementation, and Management* (New York: American Management Association, 1978), pp. 123–39.

PART IV

SYSTEM OPERATION

INTRODUCTION

Part IV of this book concentrates on several activities that are less administrative in nature than are those of Part 3; namely, performance monitoring, data base audit, and system improvement. Performance monitoring is concerned with the efficient collection of operational statistics so decisions regarding data base efficiency can be made. Data base audit focuses attention on many of the particular audit problems associated with advanced systems. System improvement looks at the establishment of threshold values beyond which some design or operational change must be made. In total, these three areas compose a very specialized but important activity of the DBA.

13

PERFORMANCE MONITORING

INTRODUCTION

Almost all data base operations require performance monitoring, because of application and data migration, to maintain a satisfactory degree of efficiency. Not only is performance monitoring necessary as an efficiency maintenance device and a system improvement tool (to be discussed in Chapter 15), but also as a prerequisite to the initial data base design. Tracking various performance parameters prior to the installation of a DBMS is difficult, at best, but can pay significant dividends to more fully insure the success of the IPS. The purpose of this chapter is to identify a wide range of performance parameters (both logical and physical), and discuss what they indicate and how they might be collected.

PERFORMANCE MEASURES

Although the area of computer performance evaluation is well developed in the literature, techniques specifically intended for data base applications are relatively limited [1]. This section will identify and discuss a number of performance parameters, many of which are well treated in the literature. Those readers requiring additional in-depth treatment are referred to Drummond [2], Ferrari [3], Hellerman and Conroy [4], and Svobodova [5].

TABLE 13.1: Data Base Performance Measures

Class	Term	Description	Monitor	Reference
Logical measure	Access probability	Relative likelihood of access; may be at attribute, aggregate or logical record level	SE	Clark [6]
	Precision	Proportion of retrieved material actually relevant	SE	Salton [7]
	Recall	Proportion of relevant material actually retrieved	SE	Salton [7]
Capacity measures	Space use	Proportion of storage space used (with or without overhead)	S	
	Redundancy	Factor indicating number of occurrences of a specific attribute value	SE	
Processor measures	Error rate	Relative number of errors	H, S	Drummond [2]
I/O	I/O requests/job	Number of I/O events per job (could be measured in terms of EXCPs)	S	MacDougall [8]
	I/O service time	Time to perform a single I/O task	H, S	MacDougall [8]
	Rotational delay (latency)	Access time delay incurred because of rotation of storage media under need/write head(s)	SP	
	Seek delay	Access time delay incurred because of mechanical movement of read/write head(s) over storage media	SP	
	Switching delay	Access time delay incurred because of channel switching from one read/write head to another	SP	

	Measure	Description	Type	Reference
CPU	Transfer rate	Number of bits or characters transferred per unit time	SP	Ferrari [3]
	Availability	Proportion of time a system is available for use	H, S	Drummond [2]
Processor Measures CPU	Average job time	Mean execution time for a representative set of jobs	S	Drummond [2]
	Hit ratio	Probability that a page (or datum) is found in some unit of storage	SE	Hellerman and Conroy [4]
	Job CPU time	Total CPU time required by a job	S	MacDougall [8]
	Number of concurrent users	Number of interactive users logged on concurrently	S	DeMeis and Weizer [9]
	Overhead	Relative amount of time spent on non-user activities	S	Ferrari [3]
	Record processing rate	Number of records processed per unit time	S	Drummond [2]
	Relative throughput	Throughput rate of base system in relation to proposed or compared system	SE	Drummond [2]
	Reliability	Probability of failure and recovery or repair within a certain time	SE	Morgan and Campbell [10]
	Response time	Turnaround time of requests or transactions in a real-time system	S	DeMeis and Weizer [9]
	Throughput	Amount of useful work completed per unit time with a given workload	S, SE	Doherty [11]
	Turnaround time	Elapsed time between submitting a job and receiving the output	S	Kimbleton [12]
	User intensity	Processing time per request/user response time	S	Shemer and Robertson [13]

Table 13.1 contains descriptions and references for data base performance measures of three classes: logical measures of system performance, measures of capacity, and processor capability (subdivided into I/O and CPU categories). This table also contains a column indicating the basic monitoring methodology: H for hardware monitor, S for software monitor, SP for specified by manufacturer/vendor (without direct user-monitoring), and SE for subjectively evaluated (perhaps with some information derived from H, S, or SP).

As was mentioned, logical measures of data base system performance are few. Essentially, there are the access probability measure, which is useful for data base design and tuning (see Chapter 7), and precision and recall, which assist in evaluating the effectiveness of search strategies and query facilities for the data base.

Measures of system storage capacity are used primarily to evaluate efficiency. In this category the two most useful parameters are space use and the amount of redundancy contained in storage. Either low space use or high redundancy should be analyzed carefully and, if not warranted for reasons of performance, should be corrected to avoid excessive operational costs.

Measures of processor efficiency are by far the most abundant; these measures are segregated into two categories: I/O and processor. The I/O category contains an indicator of accuracy of transmitted data, called error rate, and might lead to the implementation of sophisticated error correction disciplines for critical material. I/O requests per job may suggest a change in the allocation of physical devices to spread the I/O activity as evenly as possible over the available channels, and, finally, I/O service time and its individual components — seek-delay, rotational delay, switching delay, and transfer delay (a function of transfer rate and volume transmitted) — are required in a number of physical data base design algorithms (see Chapter 8).

The various measures of CPU capability are useful for a variety of data base design and operational activities. Availability indicates user application responsiveness and, therefore, service, as do number of concurrent users, response time, turnaround time, and user intensity. The physical data base design may be modified (for example, changing storage structures) to enhance these parameters. The manager of DP and the DBA both may be interested in gross measure (highly aggregated) of operational efficiency such as average job time, job CPU time, record processing rate, relative throughput, reliability, and throughput. Finally, many storage structure design methodologies depend on a measure of hit ratio to select among sequential and random processing.

METHODS OF MONITORING DATA BASE SYSTEMS

In general, there are two classes of monitors that may be effectively used on computer systems (neglecting, of course, those designated as SP and SE in Table 13.1; these are not monitors in the usual sense): hardware and software.* Table 13.2 contains a general description of both hardware and software monitors over a variety of characteristics. For most data base monitoring the software type is by far more suitable and flexible for the changing nature of the data base environment.

Navarro and Romanczuk [1] and others have suggested a particular implementation of a software monitor that serves as an interface between the DBMS and the operating system, as shown in Figure 13.1. Note the transmission of all relevant access parameters from the DBMS to the operating system. This intermediary relationship of the monitor between the DBMS and the operating system is particularly advantageous for the following reasons:

1. The individual application programs do not need to have traps inserted in them to collect data base access statistics.

2. The relatively well-defined interface between the DBMS and the operating system is all that must be modified; it simply needs to trap, for example, all calls to the data base and record attribute use.

3. The monitor can be designed to have an adjustable sampling discipline over a long period of time with little, or at least tolerable, system overhead.

4. The monitor can be modified and/or removed without affecting the application programs.

Most advanced computer systems already contain much monitoring capability, and once access is gained to the files maintained by the monitor many performance statistics can be easily obtained. IBM's System Management Facility (SMF) is one such monitor, but, as is the case with many general purpose monitors, the data obtained is highly aggregated. For example, using SMF data, one can determine the number of physical accesses to any given file by any given job (EXCPs). This does not imply, however, that each logical record contained by every physical record was required by the application program; a specialized monitor would be necessary for this purpose. One must always be careful that the statistics collected are not biased and therefore cause the data base design to be distorted.

---

*Monitors driven by firmware are certainly possible and may become common but are not generally available for a wide range of applications. See Svobodova [5] for additional information.

TABLE 13.2: Hardware/Software Monitor Characteristics

Characteristic	Hardware Monitor	Software Monitor
Ease of implementation	Requires a great deal of technical expertness to connect the monitor probes	In many situations, simply involves linking and loading a software module
Ease of interpretation	The output consists of event counts and timings; these are typically difficult to analyze	Many software monitors generate standard reports where analysis has already been done or is assisted with documentation
Effect on system overhead	No effect on machine operation	Requires machine cycles to operate and may therefore consume 1 to 10 percent (typically) of system capacity
Portability	General purpose	Written for a specific machine and operating system
Number of measures taken	Limited by number of probes	No practical limitation except overhead incurred
Types of events monitored	Generally limited to physical states of processor and I/O devices	Can monitor both physical states and logical events occuring in programs of any type

SUMMARY OF PERFORMANCE MONITORING

This chapter serves to set the stage for using the computer as a programmed assistant to the DBA. Part of this role involves keeping track of various system performance parameters that may be used either for purposes of design or simply to confirm that current operations are adequate. A taxonomy of performance measures, consisting of logical, capacity, and

FIGURE 13.1: A Software Monitor Interface for a DBMS

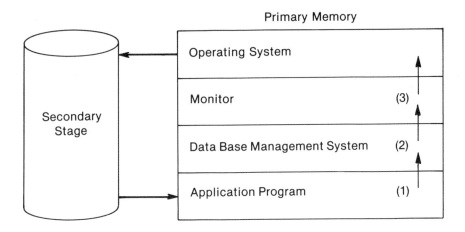

processor characteristics, has been used as a vehicle for demonstrating the wide range of uses to which operational statistics can be put. Finally, a section was devoted to the discussion of the available data collection tools, and hardware and software monitors.

REFERENCES

1. Aaron B. Navarro and Ronald J. Romanczuk, "On Monitoring Data Management Systems" (Paper presented at the ORSA/TIMS National Conference, Boston, Mass., April 22–24, 1974

2. Mansford E. Drummond, Jr., *Evaluation and Measurement Techniques for Digital Computer Systems* (Englewood Cliffs, N. J.: Prentice-Hall, 1973).

3. Domenico Ferrari, *Computer Systems Performance Evaluation* (Englewood Cliffs, N. J.: Prentice-Hall, 1978).

4. Herbert Hellerman and Thomas F. Conroy, *Computer System Performance* (New York: McGraw-Hill, 1975).

5. Liba Svobodova, *Computer Performance Measurement and Evaluation Methods: Analysis and Applications* (New York: American Elsevier, 1976).

6. Jon D. Clark, "An Attribute Access Probability Determination Procedure" (Ph.D. dissertation, Case Western Reserve University, 1977).

7. Gerard Salton, *Automatic Information Organization and Retrieval* (New York: McGraw-Hill, 1968).

8. M. H. MacDougall, "Computer System Simulation: An Introduction," *Computing Surveys* 2 (September 1970) 3: 191–209.

9. W. M. DeMeis and N. Weizer, "Measurement and Analysis of a Demand Paging Time-Sharing System," *Proceedings of the 24th ACM National Conference* (1969): 201–16.

10. D. E. Morgan and J. A. Campbell, "An Answer to a User's Plea?" *Proceedings of the First ACM-SIGME Symposium on Measurement and Evaluation* (February 1973): 112–20.

11. W. J. Doherty, "Scheduling TSO/360 for Responsiveness," *AFIPS Proceedings of the Fall Joint Computer Conference* (1970): 97–111.

12. S. R. Kimbleton, "Performance Evaluation — A Structured Approach," *AFIPS Proceedings of the Spring Joint Computer Conference* (1972): 411–16.

13. J. E. Shemer and J. B. Robertson, "Instrumentation of Time-Shared Systems," *Computer* 5 (July-August 1972): 39–48.

14

DATA BASE AUDIT

INTRODUCTION

A review of the literature and research studies on computer auditing published during the past eight years reveals one very significant point: the state-of-the-art of computer auditing trails that of information systems design by at least five years. The reasons for this gap are not clearly evident. It appears, however, that the ranks of internal and external auditors may be void of well-trained systems designers who could develop the techniques required to audit advanced information systems. Most qualified systems analysts seem to be devoting their efforts to developing new systems rather than to developing new controls and audit aids.

With the advent of even more advanced information systems (including on-line and data base applications),* the divergence between systems design technology and computer auditing will become even greater unless the following three problems are adequately solved: the need for improved systems controls, the need for effective audit techniques, and the need for increased technical proficiency for auditors. Aspects of each of these issues are discussed in this chapter.

Promises, by computer vendors, of the many benefits to be realized by acquiring the latest hardware and software have spurred management to

---

*See American Institute of Certified Public Accountants (AICPA) for a discussion of the characteristics of advanced information systems as they relate to computer auditing.

demand ambitious implementation schedules. Systems analysts and programmers are then pushed to get the systems operational, and with as much efficiency as possible. Audit controls for these systems have received very low priority because they often impede systems development and operating efficiency.

The proponent of system controls and auditability has traditionally been the internal and external auditors. With the rapid rate of systems development common in many organizations, the auditors most often arrive on the scene entirely too late to influence the systems design. Furthermore, most auditors now lack the technical proficiency to offer realistic recommendations for system controls. This point is clearly demonstrated in the current literature, where the discussions of controls for advanced systems continue to be dominated by second generation procedures such as "batch control totals" and "record counts." Creative work in developing new, effective controls for advanced systems must replace the continuing rhetoric on how to control today's systems with yesterday's techniques.

Despite the rapid development of advanced information systems, most accounting related systems have continued to provide auditors with most of the traditional audit trails and printed ledgers. Consequently, the auditor has been able to effectively audit the organization's financial statements without placing any significant reliance on the internal controls in the computer system. When testing of the computer system has been necessary, several techniques advanced in the late 1960s, including "test decks" and computer audit software, have been used.

System designs have become markedly more complex since the late 1960s; however, the computer auditing literature offers little more than a continuing debate over which technique — test decks or audit software — is most effective in various situations. With the increasing use of data base management systems, audit software packages have become nearly useless. Test decks and related control over program changes offer little satisfaction in auditing complex, integrated management information systems where program modifications represent a daily ritual during the several years of system development and implementation.

Just as in the case of system controls, radically new ideas seem to be needed if effective audit techniques are to be developed for advanced systems. The type of innovative design required must not be restricted to previous audit techniques, or even to those developed during the early generations of computer-based accounting systems. Other disciplines must be searched for relevant audit aids, just as these disciplines have been used for new approaches to information systems design. Unfortunately, the current literature on computer auditing only hints at the difficult problems facing the auditor of advanced systems and offers very little constructive assistance in coping with these problems.

The developments in system controls and audit techniques previously described will probably have to come from the group most interested in these achievements — the auditors themselves. Unfortunately, very few of today's auditors possess the technical proficiency to deal with the problems inherent in advanced systems. Apart from developing control and audit techniques for these systems, most auditors are severely limited in their ability to understand the flow of transactions through modern, complex systems — a requirement for auditing any system. These deficiencies, however, may not be the fault of the individual auditor.

Most of today's practicing auditors graduated from universities prior to the offering of data processing education other than, perhaps, a course in FORTRAN programming, which provides little insight into understanding advanced management information systems. Few, if any, data processing courses are available to practicing auditors through the course offerings of the state and national accounting societies. When courses are offered they are usually too basic and rarely deal realistically with computer auditing, especially auditing advanced systems. Even the published literature offers little assistance. Although the number of articles related to computer auditing seems to be increasing each year, most of this material contains no substance as the authors warn of undetected computer fraud and continue their debate of the pros and cons of "test decks."

The lack of helpful information for the practicing auditor may well stem from the lack of effective control and audit techniques in the first place. It is obviously difficult to develop a training course on computer auditing when the only available material has been out-of-date for at least the past several years. This puts the practicing DBA into a very difficult position; one in which there is a need, if not an expectation, for auditability (as with simple application systems), but a limited set of techniques with which to achieve it.

This chapter will review the wide range of audit techniques and make a number of suggestions that may facilitate auditability if considered at the time of data base design.

A SURVEY OF DATA BASE AUDIT TECHNIQUES

The audit techniques to be surveyed will be broken into three general classes: audit around the computer, audit through a black box, and audit through a grey box. As shown in Figure 14.1, auditing around the computer essentially ignores the existence of the computer and simply monitors inputs and outputs for correctness. Auditing through a black box in effect treats the computer as the black box from general systems theory and each input is expected to produce a specific output. This class of techniques at least

FIGURE 14.1: Data Base Audit Techniques

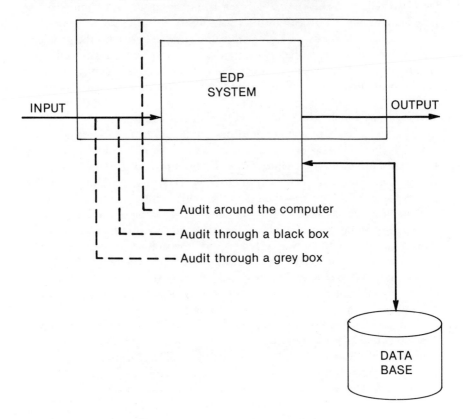

requires the acknowledgement that a computer exists and the provision of computer readable input, and in turn analyzes computer-generated output. Since the computer is treated as a black box, no knowledge of its procedures is implied. Finally, there exist grey box techniques — those whose operation requires some level of knowledge of the procedures used. As such, these techniques are the most complex and costly to develop.

Table 14.1 contains most of the audit techniques classified into these three categories, along with a brief explanation of each and several references to the literature. Each class of techniques will be discussed in the following paragraphs.

Auditing around the computer, as far as the DBA is concerned, is of little importance, since it is difficult to support an activity that largely ignores an interface with the data base. Therefore, the accounting procedures used for this class will not be discussed, although references are provided for readers who wish additional information.

TABLE 14.1: Data Base Audit Techniques

Techniques	Characteristics	References
Audit around the computer	Both popular and traditional methods of ignoring the computer; input typically monitored and output checked, but no attempt to understand procedures.	1, 3, 4, 6-11, 13, 18, 18, 26-28, 30, 36, 37, 46-48
Audit through a black box	This class of techniques also does not attempt to understand computer internal procedures but does require that computer be operated and/or assist in the audit.	1, 2, 4, 6-11, 18-24, 26-28, 30, 33, 36, 37, 46-48
Test deck	A more general and appropriate term might be "test data." This technique involves submitting artificial data, transactions, etc. and monitoring output for expected results.	16, 35, 38, 39
Concurrent processing	Detects known exception conditions and checks for output caused by them.	12
Parallel simulation	Similar to audit around the computer, but uses the computer to simulate output derived from input.	40
Controlled processing or reprocessing	Used to check for consistency of processing by submitting identical transactions a number of times or those that have already been processed.	41

(continued)

TABLE 14.1: (Continued)

Techniques	Characteristics	References
Generalized audit software	Uses general purpose programmed procedures for checking data item values, sampling, etc.; does not attempt to verify procedures. A DBMS may also be used as part of an audit package to handle more complex data structures.	5, 14, 15, 17, 25, 28, 29, 31, 33, 34, 42
Audit through a grey box	This class of techniques requires some degree of understanding of the program-internal procedures and therefore tends to be much more complex and less general-purpose than the other techniques covered.	1, 2, 4, 6-11, 13, 18-24, 26, 28, 29, 30, 37, 46-48
Integrated test facility	Operates using existing procedures but on artificial files and inputs or those physically segregated from normal operations, thus referred to as "minicompany" or "dummy company" procedure.	24, 32, 43
Tagging and tracing	Typically involves marked real data whose progress can be traced through the programmed procedures. May require changes to processing logic.	24, 43

TABLE 14.1: (Continued)

Techniques	Characteristics	References
Mapping	Monitors use of program-internal logic for excessing and/or rare use, either of which may indicate un-friendly or incorrect procedures.	23
Program code checking	Examination in detail of all processing logic, requiring a great deal of expertness both in the computer language and the application.	44
Flowchart verification	Similar to program code checking, but done at the flowchart level and, thus, is less time consuming.	23
Custom-designed computer programs	Audit software written for a specific com-puter/application com-bination. Although effi-cient once written, may impede maintenance and/or modification of ap-plications.	12, 45

The class of techniques treating the computer as a black box is of interest here. These must be used off-line or with nonproduction files. Since this class of techniques ignores program internal procedures, there is no way for the same procedures to recognize transactions or data transfers solely for the purpose of auditing (artificial transactions). Particularly in the case of controlled processing or reprocessing there is a danger of updating files twice; in a production environment this is obviously intolerable. Perhaps the safest technique of this class is the use of generalized audit software, which was very popular several years ago. Actually this is an audit aid whose sampling and retrieval capabilities are controlled by the auditor — in a sense, a decision-support system. The difficulty that this technique causes is the interface problem, because of the existence of such a wide variety of system software (including operating systems and DBMSs).

Auditing through a grey box requires a rather extensive understanding, although not a complete understanding, of the program-interval procedures; therefore, this class of techniques tends to be costly to either design or execute. The integrated test facility, and custom-designed computer programs, require a great deal of system design forethought, but if run during nonpeak production time may be quite reasonable from a execution-cost point of view. Tagging and tracing requires forethought during system design and, additionally, may be costly to execute, particularly if artificial transactions must be backed out of the system. Mapping is a very reasonable cost technique that may be executed during low system-use hours; although it may not tell the auditor as much about the systems operation. Program code checking and flowchart verification are very costly operationally, but should be done as part of any systems implementation efffort, as well as during maintenance and/or modification of systems.

DATA BASE AUDIT POTENTIALS

The data base audit picture is obscure, to say the least; many second- and third-generation techniques being applied to advanced systems, particularly data base systems, are achieving inadequate results. There is some hope, however. Three proposals are made here, each of which must be evaluated prior to application in specific cases.

One possibility, at least with regard to program validation, is the use of certified software. Primarily a concept for commercial software, whether system software or application packages, the certification might be given by an independent body capable of extensive software testing. Certification would, to a considerable extent, relieve the burdern of EDP auditors in the area of software validity. Obviously, custom systems would be nearly impossible, or prohibitive in cost, to certify if they were submitted for independent testing.

A second possibility is a standardized "audit window," a window through which the data base could be queried or sampled. Insofar as we have both standardized (principally the DBTG's DBMS) and special purpose data base systems, this concept would only likely be applied to the DBTG standardized system. By defining a specific subschema for all data to be audited, generalized packages of extensive capability but reasonable cost could be provided to DBMS users.

A third possibility is the use of techniques derived from artificial intelligence for audit purposes; there is a large body of theory available that needs only to be applied to new problems. Pattern recognition, for example, could be applied to many currently collected performance parameters to detect unusual events that indicate either the possibility of error or fraud.

To be sure, there are many other evolving technologies having audit potential in the data base area (for example, data base machine and fuzzy set theory). Here we have discussed just a few.

SUMMARY OF DATA BASE AUDIT

This chapter classified data base audit techniques. In addition to discussing many techniques, a few relatively unexplored "audit potentials" were offered. An important point to be made here is that audit methodologies must be identified and considered prior to data base design and implementation, to avoid redesign and modification costs or the possibility of incurring an audit premium resulting from an intractible data base system. The DBA is best advised to consult directly with the firm's internal and external auditors for developing audit specifications for all data base systems.

REFERENCES

1. AICPA, *Management Control and Audit of Advanced EDP Systems*, (New York, 1977).

2. AICPA, *The Auditor's Study and Evaluation of Internal Control in EDP Systems*, (New York, 1977).

3. Robert Randall, "Computer Fraud: A Growing Problem," *Management Accounting* (April 1978).

4. William E. Perry and Henry C. Warner, "Systems Auditability: Friend or Foe?" *Journal of Accountancy* (February 1978).

5. Hal J. Reneau, "Auditing in a Data Base Environment," *Journal of Accountancy* (December 1977).

6. Larry E. Rittenberg and Gordon B. Davis, "The Roles of Internal and External Auditors in Auditing EDP Systems," *Journal of Accountancy* (December 1977).

7. James I. Cash, Jr.; Andrew D. Bailey, Jr.; and Andrew B. Whinston, "A Survey of Techniques for Auditing EDP-Based Accounting Information Systems," *Accounting Review* (October 1977).

8. Ina D. Banks, "Internal Control of On-Line and Real-Time Computer Systems," *Management Accounting* (June 1977).

9. R. G. Canning, "The Importance of EDP Audit and Control," *EDP Analyzer* 15 (June 1977) 6.

10. Brandt Allen, "The Biggest Computer Frauds: Lessons for CPAs," *Journal of Accountancy* (May 1977).

11. James R. Davis, "EDP Control Means Total Control," *Management Accounting* (January 1977).

12. Carol A. Schaller, "Auditing and Job Accounting Data," *Journal of Accountancy* (May 1976).

13. Geoff Horwitz, "Needed: A Computer Audit Philosophy," *Journal of Accountancy* (April 1976).

14. A. Milton Jenkins and Ron Weber, "Using DBMS Software as an Audit Tool: The Issue of Independence," *Journal of Accountancy* (April 1976).

15. L. A. Bjork, Jr., "Generalized Audit Trail Requirements and Concepts for Data Base Applications," *IBM Systems Journal* (1975) 3.

16. A. D. Chambers, "Audit Test Packs and Computer Audit Programs," *The Computer Journal* (1975) 2.

17. Donald L. Adams, "Alternatives to Computer Audit Software," *Journal of Accountancy* (November 1975).

18. Elise G. Jancura, "Technical Proficiency for Auditing Computer Processed Accounting Records," *Journal of Accountancy* (October 1975).

19. Ron Weber, "An Audit Perspective of Operating System Security," *Journal of Accountancy* (September 1975).

20. David C. Burns and James K. Loebbecke, "Internal Control Evaluation: How the Computer Can Help," *Journal of Accountancy* (August 1975).

21. Bruce M. Greenwald and Gary Oberlander, "IRS Audits of EDP Systems," *Management Accounting* (April 1975).

22. R. G. Canning, "The Internal Auditor and the Computer," *EDP Analyzer* 13 (March 1975) 3.

23. Robert L. Stone, "Who Is Responsible for Computer Fraud?" *Journal of Accountancy* (February 1975).

24. AICPA Computer Auditing Subcommittee's Auditing Advanced EDP Systems Task Force, "Advanced EDP Systems and the Auditor's Concern," *Journal of Accountancy* (January 1975).

25. Charles R. Litecky and Ron Weber, "The Demise of Generalized Audit Software Packages," *Journal of Accountancy* (November 1974).

26. John M. Horne, "EDP Controls to Check Fraud," *Management Accounting* (October 1974).

27. J. Gregory Kunkel, "Continuous Auditing by Exception," *Management Accounting* (July 1974).

28. George H. Rittersbach and Stephen D. Harlan, Jr., "Auditing Advanced Systems," *Journal of Accountancy* (June 1974).

29. Joe Wasserman, "Selecting a Computer Audit Package," *Journal of Accountancy* (April 1974).

30. E. B. Levine, "Auditing Requirements for Advanced Systems," *Journal of Accountancy* (March 1974).

31. William J. Schroeder, "Memo on Installing a Data Base System," *Journal of Accountancy* (February 1974).

32. Barry R. Chaiken and William E. Perry, "ITF — A Promising Computer Audit Technique," *Journal of Accountancy* (February 1973).

33. Clarence O. Smith and Geraldine J. Jasper, "Using the Computer in Audit Work," *Management Accounting* (October 1972).

34. Donald L. Adams and John F. Mullarkey, "A Survey of Audit Software," *Journal of Accountancy* (September 1972).

35. Gene H. Kiefer, "Systems Auditing with Test Decks," *Management Accounting* (June 1972).

36. Edward M. Milko, "Auditing Through the Computer or Around?" *Management Accounting* (August 1970).

37. E. G. Jancurra, *Audit & Control of Computer Systems* (New York: Petrocelli, 1974).

38. A. D. Chambers, "Audit Test Packs and Computer Audit Programs," *The Computer Journal* 2 (1975).

39. D. L. Adams, "A Survey of Test Data Generators," *EDPACS* (April 1973).

40. W. C. Mair, K. W. Davis, and D. R. Wood, "Parallel Simulation — A Technique for Effective Verification of Computer Programs," *EDPACS* (April 1975).

41. D. L. Adams, "Audit Software — DYL - 250 and DYL - 260, " *EDPACS* (July 1974).

42. —— "Audit Software Requirements," *EDPACS* (November 1973).

43. H. L. Weiss, "The Use of Audit Indication and Integrated Test Facility Techniques," *EDPACS* (July 1973).

44. D. L. Adams, "Audit Review of Program Code-1," *EDPACS* (August 1975).

45. —— "SMF — An Untapped Audit Resource," *EDPACS* (September 1974).

46. Elise G. Jancurra, ed., *Computers: Auditing and Control* (New York: Petrocelli/Charter, 1977).

47. W. Thomas Porter, *EDP Controls and Auditing* (Belmont, Calif.: Wadsworth, 1974).

48. Stanford Research Institute, *Systems Audibility & Control Study* vols. 1, 2, and 3 (Altamonte Springs, Fla.: Institute of Internal Auditors, 1977).

15

SYSTEM IMPROVEMENT

INTRODUCTION

The need for system improvement can be detected during data base design whenever a compromise alternative is selected, perhaps for expediency in implementation; during data base administration and its interface with users or, perhaps, from user complaints and suggestions; during the programmer interface; and during system operation. Many of the problems encountered can be solved or improved by simply reexecuting the procedures discussed for that activity. One, however, requires additional explanation: operational efficiency.

Problems of operational efficiency are frequently encountered with data base systems; the purpose of this chapter is to outline a number of efficiency improvements, or tuning techniques, that have proven useful. A taxonomy of efficiency problems will be presented, followed by a discussion of the improvement techniques.

A TAXONOMY OF DATA BASE EFFICIENCY PROBLEMS

For the purposes of this chapter, data base efficiency problems are broken into three classes:

1. Transfer speed
   Buffer size
   Blocking factor
   Channel capacity
2. Location speed
   Seek time
   Rotational delay (and switching delay)
   Address determination scheme
3. Storage efficiency
   Redundancy
   Data compaction

Transfer speed problems are primarily the result of inappropriate buffer size, blocking factors, and/or limited channel capacity. Location speed depends on secondary storage access delays, including seek time and rotational delay, and on the address determination scheme, for example, indexing and hashing). Storage efficiency is broken into problems of redundancy and data compaction. Each of these problem areas will be discussed, and solutions tailored to each will be offered.

Transfer Speed Problems

The problem of data transfer speed has been partitioned into the major categories of buffer size, blocking factor, and channel capacity. Although there are other possible causes, these are both typical and controllable. Buffer size and blocking factor are, in a sense, related techniques that will serve cases involving clustered record processing. Consider two extreme cases. Case 1 has a sequence of requests for logical records, either randomly spaced in physical storage or whose sequence is random. In either event, there is no predictable set of logical records and, therefore, no clear physical access path, through the data base, satisfying the series of requests. Case 2 has requests that are clustered; that is, when one record has been retrieved, it is either certain or at least quite likely that the next will be required as well. In Case 2, the relative predictability of references permits buffer sizing and/or blocking to be used to advantage. The general principle being exploited is based on the fact that, providing the processing time for each record is sufficiently long (may be short in absolute time), one can overlap processing of one record with the access of the next.

Each physical record retrieved from the data base requires a buffer whose capacity matches the length. Using a single buffer, once the contents have been processed one must wait for another retrieval to be made before continuing processing. If double buffering is employed, once the contents of the first buffer have been used the second can be addressed immediately; in parallel buffer one is used for the retrieval of the third physical record. If the processing of records is extremely rapid, triple or quadruple (or more) buffering may be used. An advantage of adjusting the buffer size is that it does not require the recompilation of application programs.

Adjusting the blocking factor of logical to physical records can cause significant reductions in transfer speed. Unlike multiple buffering, blocking, for example, ten logical records into each physical record reduces the individual transfer times, whose combined delays may have been quite large, into a single delay. Once the retrieval has been completed, a sequence of logical accesses can be made without incurring any physical access delay. In the previous example involving a blocking factor of ten, delay (consisting of seek time, rotational delay, etc.) is only incurred for each group of ten logical references. (Ten is obviously an arbitrary example and, in fact, the blocking factor may be n.) Unfortunately, blocking factors must be selected at compilation time for many programming languages; therefore, changing them once implemented is quite costly. In addition, blocking factors must be consistent with the physical file characteristics and require reloading if the factor is changed.

The final variable effecting transfer speed, one that is both effective and costly to increase, is channel capacity. Typically, a data processing installation adds a channel if the existing ones are not of sufficient capacity. Since this is a very expensive solution, although in many cases an effective one, some means of predicting performance improvement is desirable. This can be done in a gross way by using analytical methods. More often, however, workload characteristics must be included in the performance model, and this calls for one of the system simulators, of which CASE (Computer-Aided System Evaluation), and SCERT (Systems and Computers Evaluation and Review Technique) are examples.* These are extremely useful for performance tuning; therefore, a section of this chapter will be devoted to them.

Location Speed

Generally, location speed of data is dependent on hardware delays and procedural delays caused by the addressing mechanisms. The hardware delays consist of seek time, rotational delay (latency), and switching delay, which is negligible and, therefore, can be ignored in most instances. The hardware delays, although important, are not as controllable as one might wish. Seek time, for example, is fixed for any given read/write head movement (although it may not be linear with respect to the number of tracks traversed), but the number of occurrences of a seek delay can be minimized

---

*CASE is marketed by Tesdata Systems; SCERT by COMPRESS, a division of Comten.

by carefully positioning records in the file being accessed. Even this attempt at intelligent design can be confounded by other concurrently executing processes requiring the same device. Nevertheless, hardware delays can be modeled, and physical data base designs adjusted, to maximize operational efficiency. The system simulators discussed later in this chapter also may be used to find tolerable physical data base design solutions.

Perhaps the most fruitful area for location-speed tuning is the selection of address determination schemes that match the basic processing requirements of the application system (for example, random or sequential) and minimize hardware delay. Although a discussion of the various schemes is beyond the scope of this book, adequate references are provided to the literature.

Storage Efficiency

Although one of the general objectives of DBMSs is to control redundancy (see Chapter 2) and thereby increase storage efficiency, among other operational characteristics, two problems remain: determining how much redundancy is appropriate, if any, and the form in which data is to be stored. The first, the appropriate amount of redundancy, has not been covered extensively by literature [18, 23]; this is of little surprise considering that, most frequently, zero redundancy is the accepted standard (except where file contention among several real-time processes is likely).

Data compaction has received much more attention both in the literature [8, 27] and in practice, primarily because of the increased use of telecommunications facilities and the direct bearing of redundant transmission of data on costs. Many of the commercial DBMSs have a data compaction utility. Data compaction techniques have also been applied to data base storage facilities, but there is a tradeoff question that must always be considered: If the compacted data must be exploded prior to use, is this more costly than storage in a more usable form? When text of a message is stored, a number of application independent techniques may be used to remove excessive blanks. If the data contains frequently repeated sequences of characters, more elaborate, application-specific coding mechanisms may be used to shorten the physical representation of the logical text. A telephone directory need not have a last name stored for each telephone number occurrence; rather, just those records at the break point from one name to another need be stored. To be sure, there is a wide variety of compaction techniques available that need only be matched with appropriate applications.

SYSTEM SIMULATORS

Although originally developed for hardware-bottleneck analysis, several computer system simulators are general enough to be of use to the DBA in the selection of alternative physical data base designs. Table 15.1 contains a brief description of three commercial packages for this purpose; others may well exist.

TABLE 15.1: Computer System Simulators

	Simulator Name		
	FOREM	CASE	SCERT
Vendor	IBM	Tesdata Systems	COMPRESS, Durcion
Minimum primary memory requirement		256K bytes	110K bytes
Input data	Data and file definitions (number of records, field size, etc.), hardware characteristics	Data and file definitions, run specifications, hardware characteristics	Data and file definitions, run specifications, hardware characteristics
Output	Reports primarily on retrieval items	Multiple reports on sequential processing, multiple programming, and real-time systems	Multiple reports on multiprogramming real-time, time sharing, report use, and miscellaneous other reports

CASE was originally developed at Control Data Corporation, at a reported cost of $8 million. SCERT predates CASE by about seven years, and was the first such package available. It was developed by two people at RCA for about $2 million and was later sold to COMPRESS. FOREM was developed by IBM, but has not achieved the commercial success of either CASE or SCERT.

All require a number of parameters describing the data, file, processes, and the hardware/software environment. The output of the simulators is volume and relative loading of the various hardware components and measures of throughput. By selectively changing the workload, hardware/software, and/or other parameters, one can affect such things as throughput and configuration cost. Particularly with regard to CASE and SCERT, this endeavor is both costly and effective in predicting actual changes in performance.

SUMMARY OF SYSTEM IMPROVEMENT

The need for system improvement may come from the user or from the programmer, or as a result of performance monitoring or audit. In many cases the originally used design methods or algorithms can be reexecuted to correct the recently defined deficiencies. This chapter has covered several topics relating to performance tuning that typically occur in data base systems prior to major overhaul. These techniques can improve efficiency even on implemented systems without affecting logical procedures. Included in this chapter is a discussion of system simulators, which can be used to either improve existing systems or to try out proposed designs prior to implementation.

REFERENCES

1. S. R. Arora and W. T. Dent, "Randomized Binary Search Technique," *Communications of the ACM* 12 (February 1969) 2: 77-80.

2. Burton H. Bloom, "Space-Time Trade-offs in Hash Coding with Allowable Errors," *Communications of the ACM* 13 (July 1970) 7: 422-26.

3. Edward G. Coffman, Jr. and J. Eve, "File Structures Using Hashing Functions," *Communications of the ACM* 13 (July 1970) 7: 427-36.

4. Edward G. Coffman, Jr., L. A. Klimko and B. Ryan, "An Analysis of Seek Times in Disk Systems," *SIAM Journal on Computing* 1 (1972) 3: 269-79.

5. Satki P. Ghosh and Michael E. Senko, "File Organization—On the Selection of Random Access Index Points for Sequential Files," *Journal of the ACM* 16 (October 1969) 4: 569-79.

6. Leo H. Groner and Amrit L. Goel, "Concurrency in Hashed File Access," *Information Processing-74*, North-Holland, pp. 431-5.

7. Aaron Gurski, "A Note on the Analysis of Keys for Use in Hashing," *BIT* 13 (1973) 1: 120-22.

8. Bruce Hahn, "A New Technique for Compression and Storage of Data," *Communications of the ACM* 17 (August 1974) 8: 434-36.

9. Gary D. Knott, "Hashing Functions and Hash Table-Storage and Retrieval," *Computer Journal* 18 (August 1975) 3: 265-78.

10. Vincent Y. Lum, "General Performance Analysis of Key-to-Address Transformation Methods Using an Abstract File Concept," *Communications of the ACM* 16 (October 1973) 10: 603-12.

11. Vincent Y. Lum and P. S. T. Yuen, "Additional Results on Key-to-Address Transform Techniques: A Fundamental Performance Study on Large Existing Formatted Files," *Communications of the ACM* 15 (November 1972) 11: 996-97.

12. Vincent Y. Lum, P. S. T. Yuen and M. Dodd, "Key-to-Address Transformation Techniques—A Fundamental Performance Study on Large Existing Formatted Files," *Communications of the ACM* 14 (April 1971) 4: 238-39.

13. W. D. Maurer and T. G. Lewis, "Hash Table Methods," *ACM Computing Surveys* 7 (March 1975) 1: 5-20.

14. James K. Mullin, "Retrieval-Update Speed Trade-offs Using Combined Indexes," *Communications of the ACM* 14 (December 1971) 12: 775-76.

15. William W. Peterson, "Addressing for Random Access Storage," *IBM Journal of Research and Development* 1 (April 1957) 2: 130-46.

16. V. K. Premchand, "Some Aspects of Buffering," *Journal of the Computer Society of India* 4 (January 1974) 1: 8-14.

17. G. Schay, Jr., and N. Raver, "A Method for Key-to-Address Transformations," *IBM Journal of Research and Development* 7 (April 1963) 2: 121-26.

18. Eugene S. Schwartz, "A Dictionary for Minimum Redundancy Encoding," *Journal of the ACM* 10 (October 1963) 4: 413-39.

19. Michael E. Senko, Vincent Y. Lum and P. J. Owens, "A File Organization Evaluation Model (FOREM)," *Information Processing-68*, North-Holland, pp. C19-28.

20. Dennis G. Severance, "Identifier Search Mechanisms, A Survey and Generalized Model," *ACM Computing Surveys* 6 (September 1974) 3: 173-94.

21. Dennis G. Severance and A. G. Merten, "Performance Evaluation of File Organizations Through Modeling," *Proceedings of the 27th National Conference, ACM* (1972): 1061-72.

22. C. E. Skinner, "Effects of Storage Contention on System Performance," *IBM Systems Journal* 8 (1969) 4: 319-33.

23. Joel R. Sklaroff, "Redundancy Management Technique for Space Shuttle Computers," *IBM Journal of Research and Development* 20 (January 1976) 1: 20-30.

24. Daniel Teichroew, "Computer Simulation-Discussion of the Technique and Comparison of Languages," *Communications of the ACM* 9 (October 1966) 10: 723-41.

25. R. E. Wagner, "Indexing Design Considerations," *IBM Systems Journal* 12 (December 1973) 4: 351-67.

26. S. J. Waters, "Estimating Magnetic Disk Seeks," *Computer Journal* 18 (February 1974) 1: 17-24.

27. D. A. Huffman, "A Method for the Construction of Minimum-Redundancy Codes," *Proceedings of I.R.E.* 40 (September 1950): 1068.

28. Gio Wiederhold, *Database Design* (New York: McGraw-Hill, 1977), 55-57.

PART V

IMPLEMENTATION

INTRODUCTION

Having discussed in detail the essential terms and concepts of data base systems, their design, administration, and operation, Part V's objective is threefold: to outline the basic decision (whether a DBMS will be a benefit in a particular situation), to develop a generalized implementation plan, and to provide a discussion of the future of data base technology. Chapter 16 assists the reader in evaluating the relative benefit of data base operation, with due consideration for both advantages and disadvantages, including implementation costs. Chapter 17 develops a step-by-step implementation plan to facilitate an easy transition from a conventional file-processing environment to one with a DBMS. Finally, Chapter 18 outlines a number of likely advancements in data base technology that will make it exploitable by a larger set of users.

16

THE IMPLEMENTATION DECISION

INTRODUCTION

To decide intelligently whether to implement a DBMS, one must consider the advantages and disadvantages outlined in Chapter 2 in light of the
existing or proposed operational environment. This chapter will begin by
reviewing the advantages and disadvantages of DBMS, but rather than a
discussion (as in Chapter 2) of the issues, questions will be asked whose
answers might determine the relevance of each in a particular case. Following this are the results of a survey of DBAs regarding many important
points for the question of data base implementation.

A REVIEW OF DBMS ADVANTAGES AND DISADVANTAGES

Any cost/benefit analysis of a DBMS must carefully weigh all changes
that may accrue from the rather significant change in processing
methodology. Chapter 2 laid the groundwork of factors to be considered,
both those of benefits and of costs. Although this taxonomy is not exit does provide the reader with, at least, general classes of benefits and costs
to be considered. The list below contains the same classification presented
in Chapter 2, but with the addition of a number of questions (not
exhaustive) whose answers should assist DP management in deciding for or

against a DBMS. The questions have been asked in such a way that "yes" answers to points in the advantages section lead to the notion of implementing a DBMS; "no" answers, to the points in the disadvantages counter to this notion.

Advantages
User-directed

1. Complexity of Relationships
Do anticipated applications have complex data requirements?
Will users from various organizational areas be using the same data?
2. Centralized Control of Data
Is there currently a problem with redundant data?
Do errors easily propogate through the system?
Are current security and integrity controls ineffective?
Is restart/recovery an unthinkable task?
3. Ease of Search
Do users require a less procedural, perhaps on-line, query facility?
Are unanticipated questions delayed because there is no way to process them?
Do users complain about simple, one-time, questions not being answerable from machine-stored data?

Operational

1. Controlled Redundancy
Is system maintenance difficult due to undocumented redundancy?
Is there confusion among users regarding data meaning, content, etc.?
2. Independence
Must application programs be modified when device changes are made?
Do even minor changes in data description require program modification and recompilation?
3. Accessibility
Is there a need for real-time access to data, particularly to shared data?
Are user lock-outs from data due to file contention affecting system performance?
4. Ease of Creating, Restructuring, Updating, and Maintaining
Would pre-programmed integrated aids for these activities help production?
5. Flexibility
Can unanticipated queries be easily processed?
Can changes to the data base or applications be implemented efficiently?

Disadvantages
Costs
1. Initial
Can 30-150K dollars be spent on a software system?
Can additional monies (probably a great deal) be allocated to system conversion and development?
2. Continuing
Will users tolerate an estimated 20% increase in production costs?
Is there sufficient technical expertise to handle the frequent problems likely to be encountered as with any complex piece of software?
Complexity
Does the future DP budget have enough headroom for the specialized personnel (systems and application programmers) required at a DBMS installation?
Can the required staff be hired and retained?
User Indoctrination
Are the potential users capable and willing to change their traditional views of DP, new DBMS capabilities, and their responsibility to the systems?
Will the concept of "users own data" be difficult to break?
Is there a historical precedent for the separation of functions which will be integrated?
Likelihood of Success
Is top management providing not only financial support but also moral support?
Are sufficient resources being allocated to rethinking older generation systems and their continued role when a DBMS is implemented?

It would be comforting to think that a more formal, perhaps mathematical, procedure for cost/benefit analysis could be used (perhaps like Joslin's [1] cost-value technique). Unfortunately, many of the important advantages of DBMS are not quantifiable, if not intangible; therefore, the costs may frequently outweigh the benefit because of the limitations of the analysis procedure. The purpose of this section is to assist DP management in considering fully all of the relevant factors in a given situation.

A PRAGMATIC VIEW OF THE DBMS PAYOFF

Wiorkowski and Wiorkowski [2] did a survey of 27 sites with DBMSs using a variety of commercial systems and hardware configurations. In addition, the survey included industrial groups from retailing, manufacturing, insurance, financing, banking, government, and education. The contact with each was made through the DBA, or the functional equivalent, by telephone. Tables 16.1 and 16.2 contain, respectively, the DBA's ratings of

TABLE 16.1: DBA Ratings of DBMS Advantages

Category	Rating
Data independence	4.4
Data integrity	4.3
On-line operation	4.0
Centralized control	3.8
Ease and flexibility in restructuring and maintaining data	3.7
Reduction in data redundancy	3.6
Integrated applications (complex relationships)	3.5
Quick handling of unanticipated requests (unstructured query)	3.5
Programmers not having to know physical structure	3.5
Security and privacy	3.1

TABLE 16.2: DBA Ratings of DBMS Disadvantages

Category	Rating
Operational inefficiency	2.8
Additional operating cost	2.4
Cost of additional hardware/software	2.3
User problems during transition	2.2
Cost of the DBMS	2.1
Cost of installing DBMS	2.0
Additional cost of storing data	2.0

the advantages and disadvantages scored on a five point scale, five being high and one being low. The taxonomies (that of Chapter 2 and Wiorkowski and Wiorkowski) are roughly equivalent, and the contents of each table have been rank ordered.

For a full discussion of each of the advantages and disadvantages contained in these tables the reader is referred to Wiorkowski and Wiorkowski [2]. There are, however, a few obvious points that deserve mention here. First, although programmers need not know the physical structure of data to the same extent as in a conventional file processing environment, problems of efficiency may arise if they don't have this knowledge. Second, security and privacy (particularly privacy) may have received the lowest score (3.1), but it is likely to become higher if HR 1984 ever comes out of committee.* Finally, the additional cost of storing data (a disadvantage) is a likely outgrowth of system flexibility; such as the links and pointers used to provide extensive logical capability must be stored as data, thus leading very frequently to large files. It is not surprising, then, that this survey found average operational costs increased 25 percent after the installation of a DBMS.

SUMMARY OF THE DATA BASE IMPLEMENTATION DECISION

Whether a DBMS will be cost-effective in a given situation depends on a number of tangible and intangible factors. This chapter has outlined many of the factors to be considered and presented the results of a survey of DBAs regarding their perception of the advantages and disadvantages. It should be clear, both from the literature and the DBA comments presented, that the installation of a DBMS is not a panacea for general DP problems; it has a place and it should be applied only where warranted.

REFERENCES

1. E. O. Joslin, *Computer Selection* (Fairfax Station, Va.: Technology Press, 1977).

2. Gabrielle K. Wiorkowski and John J. Wiorkowski, "Does a Data Base Management System Pay Off?" *Datamation* 24 (April 1978) 4: 109–14.

---

*HR 1984 is the private sector equivalent of the Security Act of 1974, which has been in committee for several years.

17

DEVELOPING AN IMPLEMENTATION PLAN

INTRODUCTION

An implementation plan is inextricably related to the organization in which the implementation is being made. Because of this there is very little in the literature regarding the particular problems of implementing a data base system [1]. It has been recognized, however, that the success of any system is highly dependent on the implementation procedures carried out [2]; therefore, this chapter will attempt to provide some guidance on the subject. As in past chapters, a taxonomy of factors to be considered will be presented along with a discussion of each.

A TAXONOMY OF IMPLEMENTATION TASKS

The taxonomy of data base implementation tasks to be used in this chapter consists of four categories: planning, DBMS implementation, preapplication development, and application development. The planning category consists of tasks that are typically performed once during the implementation of the DBMS, but prior to receiving the DBMS and related hardware/software support systems. Subsequent to the planning stage, the DBMS-required hardware/software modifications are made. Having completed this stage the two applications-oriented stages can be entered. The first, the preapplication development stage, consists primarily of data definitions at the schema and subschema levels. Entries here may occur, in some cases, prior to application system development, but with due consideration for the systems that are proposed. The final stage, application development, will recur frequently as new systems are defined, but, for the data base implementation use set out here, applications conversion must also be considered.

The following list contains many of the generally applicable tasks required for data base implementation. Not only are the steps classified according to the previously discussed taxonomy, but relevant points about each are also included:

Data Base Planning

1. Appoint DBA to spearhead implementation effort and add additional staff as necessary.

2. Set up organizational steering committee, including user-group representation and technical and corporate support.

3. Determine what existing systems will be converted for immediate application on the proposed data base.

4. Generate new systems development schedule.

5. Select DBMS that meets current and future needs and allows flexibility for tentative future systems.

6. Determine hardware/software enhancements necessary to effectively handle increased overhead of DBMS and necessary changes in applications.

7. Allocate staff (systems analysis and programming) to generate initial DD/D; this can and should be done well in advance of DBMS installation.

8. Develop conversion plan for existing application systems on enhanced hardware/software.

9. Assign available resources to new system development.

10. Train system and application programmers in data base methods.

11. Hire additional personnel as necessary; some experienced classifications are very difficult to obtain in the marketplace.

12. Indoctrinate users in new capabilities, responsibilities, and costs characteristic of DBMS.

DBMS Implementation

1. Carry out hardware upgrade, if necessary.

2. Perform software upgrade (particularly the operating system) if necessary. This may require a significant amount of change to the existing system's job control language (JCL).

3. Generate the DBMS software system, including DD/D if it is integrated.

4. Generate the DD/D if of stand-alone or passive type.

5. Load the data base and DD/D for purposes of system test. Several application types and their required data bases will probably be sufficient.

6. System test. This is a good opportunity for system and application programmers to gain experience in data base operation.

Preapplication Development

1. Define and load schema definitions.

2. Define and load subschema definitions as they are generated.

3. Define and load all other data, and process definitions to be maintained in the DD/D.

4. Convert data.

Application Development

1. Convert existing applications with due regard for the subschema definition provided by the DBA.

2. Test applications.

3. Update application documentation and submit required changes to the DD/D.

4. Turn application system over to production having approval of DP and the DBA.

SUMMARY OF DBMS IMPLEMENTATION

As with any change in technology, it is easy, if not typical, to underestimate the level of difficulty involved in the conversion and transition process; the change from conventional file processing to a data base system environment requires some dramatic and some subtle modifications to the system analysis, design, selection, test, and implementation process. It is critical that this endeavor be considered carefully and be supported by top management; otherwise, failure is likely to occur. This chapter has classified the DBMS implementation process into four stages: planning, DBMS implementation, preapplication, and application development. Each was outlined and suggestions offered regarding important considerations.

REFERENCES

1. Leo J. Cohen, "Data Base Considerations and Implementation Techniques," *Data Management*, September 1972, pp 40–45.

2. Howard L. Morgan and John V. Soden, "Understanding MIS Failures," *Data Base* 5 (Winter 1973) 2, 3, 4: 157–71.

18

THE FUTURE OF DATA BASE

INTRODUCTION

This book has attempted to paint as unbiased a picture of data base technology as possible, offering clear statements of both advantages and disadvantages (see Chapter 2). Unfortunately, as with management information systems, data base has been oversold. Without a doubt, it is called for and appropriate in some situations; in others it becomes a disaster of increased costs. There are a number of advances both in hardware and software systems that may alleviate the oversell problem and another that will enhance applications involving untrained users.

HARDWARE DEVELOPMENTS

Two hardware developments likely to have a beneficial impact on computer system efficiency when a DBMS is used are data base machine [1, 2] and associative processing [3]. Data base machine offers significant cost-performance improvement, sometimes as high as ten to one, over using the central processor for the same data base access. This is accomplished by using a dedicated and specialized computer to handle many of the repetitive tasks required whenever a call to the data base is made, but at a much faster rate and, perhaps more important, without occupying the main computer's resources while the call is being accomplished. Such tasks as error checking, concurrent update, and encryption can easily and efficiently be handled through the data base machine. Figure 18.1 contains an example architecture of a data base machine used as a back end. Note that it is driven by the I/O processor, which may also use a front end such as a communications controller.

FIGURE 18.1: A Data Base Machine Architecture

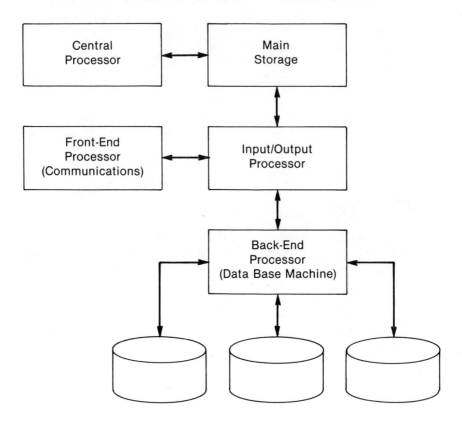

Associative processors address data by content, rather than by physical locations. Conventional processors access data on a bit-parallel word-serial basis, thus requiring either knowledge of a specific physical address or a serial scan of all addresses. Associative memory (a component of an associative processor) accesses data on a word-paralled bit-serial basis; each bit of every word in memory is scanned simultaneously, subject to some search criterion. If it satifies the criterion, a bit is set to so indicate,

FIGURE 18.2: An Associative Processor Architecture

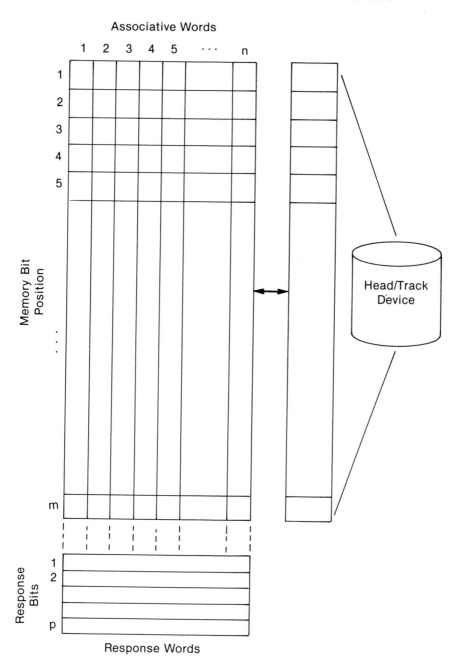

Associative Words

1 2 3 4 5 · · · n

Memory Bit Position

Head/Track Device

Response Bits

Response Words

and the second bit position (see Figure 18.2) of all the previously selected words is scanned, and the response bit again is set for those satisfying the criterion. When the search is completed, another instruction may be applied to all words simultaneously to cause any general data processing operation (such as add, subtract, and write). Since the associative memory is not sufficiently large to store an entire data base, a segment of it will be moved in, operated on, followed by the remaining segments of the data base.

SOFTWARE DEVELOPMENTS

The relational data model (see Chapter 4), advocated originally by Codd [4] and now many others, has primarily been criticized because of problems of efficiency of the relatively few implemented versions. The logical advantages of this model are simply too great for it to be ignored once the retrieval efficiency problem is solved. Fortunately both the data base machine concept and the associative processor will improve efficiency markedly; only the costs must be reduced, which is a near certainty with LSI technology.

The relational model also includes a nonprocedural query language; many of these are currently under development and promise wide application advantages to untrained, middle-, and top-level managers of all types. A language of this type (SQL [5]) has been reported with respect to the potential and actual human factor advantages [6] over more procedural languages.

SUMMARY OF THE FUTURE OF DATA BASE

The advances resulting from data base machine, associative processing, and nonprocedural languages that are part of the relational model are clearly significant. The role of the DBA is likely to change as well. Already the explosive growth in the number of different commercial systems is leveling off (except for mini- and micro-computers) and the concepts driving the various implementations are beginning to stablize and mature to the point where the DBA may devote more effort to administration than to system programming.

REFERENCES

1. E. A. Ozkarahan, S. A. Schuster, and K. C. Smith, "RAP — An Associative Processor for Data Base Management," *AFIPS Conference Proceedings* (1975): 379–87.

2. R. H. Canaday, R. D. Harrison, E. L. Ivie, J. L. Ryder, and L. A. Wehr, "A BackEnd Computer for Data Base Management," *Communications of the ACM* 17 (October 1974) 10: 575–82.

3. David K. Hsiao and Stuart E. Madnick, "Database Machine Architecture in the Context of Information Technology Evaluation," *Proceedings of the 3rd International Conference on Very Large Data Bases,* October 1977.

4. E. F. Codd, "A Relational Model of Data for Large Shared Data Banks," *Communications of the ACM* 13 (June 1970) 6: 377–87.

5. C. Welty, *SQL Manual* (Amherst, Mass.: University of Massachusetts, November 1978).

6. C. Welty and D. W. Stemple, "A Human Factors Comparison of a Procedural and Nonprocedural Query Language," *COINS Technical Report 78-23* (December 1978).

APPENDIX A

A FEATURE ANALYSIS OF DBMSs

Name	Vendor	Approximate Number of Users	Computers Supported	Operating Systems Supported	Minimum Memory Requirement	DD/D Support
ADABAS	Software AG of North America	>300	IBM S/360,370, and most compatible machines, Siemens 4004	DOS, DOS/VS, OS, OS/VS, EDOS	200 bytes	YES
DATACOM/DB	Applied Data Research	>100	IBM S/360,370, and most compatible machines	DOS, DOS/VS, OS, OS/VS, MUS, EDOS, DOS/USE	32K bytes	YES
DBMS-10	Digital Equipment	>60	DEC-10	TOPS 10	32K words	NO
DBMS-20	Digital Equipment	>60	DEC-20	TOPS 20	32K words	NO
DL/1	IBM	>550	IBM S/370 model 125, and up, 4300 series	DOS/VS, DOS/USE	90K bytes	NO
DM-IV/IDS-II	Honeywell	>160	Honeywell Series 60, 600, 6000, and Level 66	G-COS	12K words	YES
DMS-II	Burroughs	>400	B700, B800	MCP	180K bytes	YES
DMS/90	Sperry Univac	>50	Univac 90	OS/3; VS/9	80K bytes	YES
DMS 1100	Sperry Univac	>500	1100 Series	EXEC 8	15K words	YES

DPL	National Information Systems	>60	DEC-10, DEC-20	TOPS-10 TOPS-20	96K words	YES
DRS/XBS	A.R.A.P.	>85	IBM 1130 and S/370, DEC-11	OS/VS, TSO, VM/CMS; IAS, RSX-11, DNA/TSO	IBM 1130 32K bytes S/370 180K bytes DEC-11 64K bytes	YES
IDMS	Cullinane	>500	IBM S/360, 370; 303X, 4300 series	DOS, DOS/VS, OS, OS/VS, MUS	65K bytes	YES
IMS	IBM	>1000	IBM S/360, 370, 303X	IMS-2-OS, OS/VS; IMS/VS-OS/VS	128K bytes	YES
INQUIRE	Infodata Systems	>100	IBM S/360 model 40 and larger; S/370 model 135 and larger, and most compatibles	OS, OS/VS, CMS, MVS	40K bytes	YES
MODEL 204	Computer Corporation of America	>40	IBM S/360, S/370, and most compatibles	OS, OS/VS, MUS	280K bytes	YES
RAMIS	Mathematica Products Group	>1000	IBM S/360, S/370 and most compatibles	OS, OS/VS, DOS/VS, TSO, VM, CMS	160K bytes	YES
SYSTEM 2000	MRI Systems	>700	IBM S/360, S/370; Amdal 470, Univac 100, CDC Cyber Series	OS, OS/VS, CMS, DOS/VS, MUS, EXEC 8; NOS	180K bytes (IBM) 32K words (Univac) 20K words (CDC)	YES
TOTAL	CINCOM Systems	>2300	Most	Most	40K bytes on S/360 S/370	YES

APPENDIX B

ANNOTATED BIBLIOGRAPHY OF
DATA BASE DESIGN AIDS

Astrahan, M. M. and Chamberlin, D. D. "Implementation of a Structured English Query Language." *Communications of the ACM* 18 (1975) 10: 580–88. An interpreter for SEQUEL is described that minimizes data accessing operations required to respond to an arbitrary query.

Babad, Jair M. "A Record and File Partitioning Model." *Communications of the ACM* 20 (1977) 1: 22-31. Presents both nonlinear and mixed integer programming solutions that have generated designs resulting in storage and transfer cost savings of 70 percent.

Benner, Frank H. "On Designing Generalized File Records for Management Information Systems." *AFIPS Fall Joint Computer Conference* 31 (1967): 291–304. Several phases of the overall technique, at the time of writing, were implemented and resulted in an improvement in storage use.

Blasgen, M. W. and Eswaran, K. P. "Storage and Access in Relational Data Base." *IBM Systems Journal* 16 (1977) 4: 363–77. Four techniques for evaluating a general query are compared relative to the cost of accessing secondary storage. These techniques are compared numerically and analytically for various values of important parameters.

Bloom, Burton H. "Some Techniques and Trade-Offs Affecting Large Data Base Retrieval Times." *Proceedings of the 24th National Conference, ACM*(1969): 83–95. Presents a theoretical analysis of certain techniques for organizing large amounts of stored data and the retrieval time/file maintenance tradeoff.

Cardenas, Alfonso F. "Analysis and Performance of Inverted Data Base Structures." *Communications of the ACM* 18 (1975) 5: 253–63. Formulations are derived to estimate average access time (read only) and storage requirements, formalizing the interaction of data base content characteristics, logical complexity of queries, and machine timing and blocking specifications identified as having a first-order effect on performance.

Cardenas, Alfonso F. "Evaluation and Selection of File Organization—A Model and System." *Communications of the ACM* 16 (1973) 9: 540–48. Employs a design methodology, a model, and a programmed system that estimates storage costs and average access times. An actual test of the methodology was described.

Casey, R. G. "Design of Tree Structures for Efficient Querying." *Communications of the ACM* 16 (1973) 9: 549–56. Discusses a heuristic that designs optimal tree structures although ordinarily the optimal tree cannot be implemented by means of practical techniques. An application of this technique was not reported.

Chandy, K. M., and Ramamoorthy, C. V. "Optimization of Information Storage Systems." *Information and Control* 13 (1968) 6: 509–26. Describes a method of selecting an optimum subset of memory types and the sizes of each to minimize average access time. A realistic implementation was not cited.

Chow, David K. "New Balanced-File Organization Schemes." *Information and Control* 15 (1969): 377–96. Compares several balanced file organization schemes from a theoretical point of view.

Chu, Wesley W. "Optimal File Allocation in a Multiple Computer System." *IEEE Transactions on Computers* C-18 (1970) 19: 885–89. Presents a linear integer zero-one programming solution to the file allocation problem applied to a multiple computer system. A single example of its application was discussed.

Clapson, Philip. "Improving the Access Time for Random Access Files." *Communications of the ACM* 20 (1977) 3: 127–35. Presents a model for improving the performance of hashing and some empirical results of an experiment.

Clark, Jon D. "An Attribute Access Probability Determination Procedure." Ph.D. dissertation, Case Western Reserve University, 1977. A forms-driven technique that assumes either the availability of COBOL code or the ability to estimate attribute use. It has been used in a practical setting and could easily be modified to handle other programming languages and, with some additional development, be automated.

Coffman, E. G. and Bruno, J. "On File Structuring for Non-Uniform Access Frequencies." *Nordisk Behandlings Informations Tedskrift* 10 (1970): 443–56. Considers methods for structuring files so that initially unknown but nonuniform access frequencies are exploited in a way that reduces mean search times.

Collmeyer, A. J., and Shemer, J. E. "Analysis of Retrieval Performance for Selected File Organization Techniques." *AFIPS, Fall Joint Computer Conference* 37 (1970): 201–10. Comparison of spatial, calculated, and tabular index methods relative to access time using a hypothetical case. This technique assumes a uniprogramming environment.

Dearnly, P. "A Model of a Self-Organizing Data Management System." *The Computer Journal* 17 (1974) 1: 13–16. Reports on a self-organizing tool that not only selects access methods but also physical data record designs. A test case was briefly described.

Eisner, Mark J. and Severance, Dennis G. "Mathematical Techniques for Efficient Record Segmentation in Large Shared Databases." *Journal of the Association for Computing Machinery* 23 (1976) 4: 619–35. This technique for partitioning data into primary and secondary record segments can be applied to both unprogramming and multiprogramming systems. The algorithms have been applied to numerous problems, some resulting in a reduction of total system cost by 65 percent.

Gerritsen, Rob "A Preliminary System for the Design of DBTG Data Structures." *Communications of the ACM* 18 (1975) 10: 551–57. Using a hierarchically structured nonprocedural language, queries are entered interactively into the programmed system, which then produces the minimal set of data structures. The system was not reported on in an actual test case.

Hall, P. A. V. "Optimization of Single Expressions in a Relational Data Base System." *IBM Journal of Research and Development* (May 1976): 244–57. This paper examines the optimization of a single query defined by a relational algebra. Measurements of an experimental data base showed improvements in execution time with a small overhead for optimization.

Hoffer, Jeffrey A. "A Clustering Approach to the Generation of Subfiles for the Design of a Computer Data Base." Ph.D. dissertation, Cornell University, 1975. A zero-one nonlinear programming solution using branch and bound that may be used in conjunction with a clustering algorithm to increase computational feasibility. The model assumes, among other things, that there is no contention for the physical records. These algorithms have been implemented and used in practical settings.

IBM. "Time Automated Grid System (TAG): Sales and Systems Guide." White Plains, N.Y.: International Business Machines, Technical Publication GY20-0358-1, 2nd ed. (May 1971). A method of information requirements specification that, unlike similar techniques, considers the time dimension of data and can thereby determine a variety of file requirements. This has not proved to be a commercial success.

Lum, V. Y. "Multi-Attribute Retrieval with Combined Indexes." *Communications of the ACM* 13 (1970) 11: 660–65. Through the use of redundancy and storing keys that satisfy different combinations of secondary index values in "buckets," it is shown to be possible to retrieve all keys satisfying any input query derived from a subset of fields by a single access to an index file, although each bucket may be used for many combinations of values and a combination of buckets may be required for a given query.

Lum, V. Y. and Ling, H. "An Optimization Problem on the Selection of Secondary Keys." *Proceedings of the 26th National Conference, ACM* (1971): 349–56. A mathematical solution to the problem of selecting the optimal set of keys on which to index a file is presented. FOREM (A File Organization Evaluation Model by IBM) was used for a test application.

Lum, V. Y.; Ling, H.; and Senko, M. E. "Analysis of a Complex Data Management Access Method by Simulation Modeling." *AFIPS, Fall Joint Computer Conference* 37 (1970): 211–22. Presents an alternative to typical parametric studies that saves several orders of magnitude in computational costs and uses FOREM I. The example involves an indexed sequential access method.

Lum, V. Y.; Yuen, P. S. T.; and Dodd, M. "Key-to-Address Transform Techniques: A Fundamental Performance Study on Large Existing Formatted Files." *Communications of the ACM* 14 (1971) 4: 228–39. Presents the results of a study of eight key-to-address transformation methods. Practical guidelines are developed for their selection.

Maxwell, W. L., and Severance, D. G. "Comparison of Alternatives for the Representation of Data Item Values in an Information System." *Data Base* 5 (1973) 2, 3, 4: 121–39. Reports on various ways of physically representing data to increase the rate at which useful data

can be made available to an application program. An artificial example
was discussed.

Milman, Y. "An Approach to Optimal Design of Storage Parameters in
Databases." *Communications of the ACM* 20 (1977) 5: 347–50. After
identifying the critical design factor as being either storage space or
number of accesses, proceeds to derive an optimal solution. The technique was not validated in an actual data base environment.

NCR. "A Study Guide for Accurately Defined Systems." Dayton, Ohio:
National Cash Register Co., 1968. Provides a methodology for determining complete and consistent information requirements for user applications. Begins by defining output and finally tracing each back to
the required inputs, procedures, etc. This was not a commercial success, because of the very high labor intensity.

Patt, Yale N. "Variable Length Tree Structures Having Minimum Average
Search Time." *Communications of the ACM* 12 (1969) 2: 72–76. A procedure is developed for constructing a tree with a minimum average
search time. A simple closed expression for this minimum average
search time is obtained as a function of the number of terminal modes;
storage capacity is also determined. An actual implementation was not
cited.

Raver, N., and Hubbard, G. U. "Automated Logical Data Base Design:
Concepts and Applications." *IBM Systems Journal* 16 (1977) 3:
287–312. One of the few commercially available tools (IBM's Data Base
Design Aid) for analyzing data requirements, suggesting a logical
design and providing quality control for the experienced designer.

Rothnie, James B., and Lozano, Tomas. "Attribute Based File Organization in a Paged Memory Environment." *Communications of the ACM*
17 (1974) 2: 63–69. Attempts to heuristically minimize page accesses
assuming multiple key hashing. Apparently was not applied in live data
base environment.

Schkolnick, Mario. "A Clustering Algorithm for Hierarchical Structures."
ACM Transactions on Database Systems 2 (March 1977) 1: 27–44. A
very fast algorithm that determines the optimal partitions of a tree
structure is described. The algorithm has been used to determine the
best partitions of an IMS-type tree into data set groups as well as to
evaluate the costs of different alternatives.

Senko, M. E.; Ling, H.; Lum, V. Y.; Meadow, H. R.; Bryman, M. R.;

Drake, R. J.; and Meyer, B. C. *File Design Handbook*. Submitted to Rome Air Development Center, Air Force Systems Command, Griffiss Air Force Base, New York, by IBM, San Jose Research Laboratory, San Jose, California, and Federal Systems Division, Gaithersburg, Maryland, November 1969. (Contract AF 30602–69–C–0100). A design methodology is defined that gives close-to-optimal accessing configurations by access method and file size.

Senko, M. E.; Lum, V. Y.; and Owens, P. J. "A File Organization Evaluation Model (FOREM)." *Information Processing-68*, North Holland, pp. C19–C28. Reports on a File Organization Evaluation Model (FOREM) that is designed for simulation of management inquiry systems and specifically with file content and query-dependent variable volume transaction problems.

Severance, D. G., and Carlis, J. V. "A Practical Approach to Selecting Record Access Paths." *Computing Surveys* 9 (1977) 4: 259–72. Based on requirements of speed of response, volume of on-line update, and quantity of records retrieved, selects, though with some discretion, the most appropriate access path. Verification of the method was primarily experiential and proved to be practical and low cost.

Severance, D. G., and Merten, A. G. "Performance Evaluation of File Organizations through Modeling." *Proceedings of the 27th National Conference, ACM* (1972): 1061–72. A simulation model is used to generate a range of alternative file organizations by varying the parameters of a generalized model. These organizations are evaluated in terms of retrieval, storage space, and maintenance overhead.

Shneiderman, Ben. "Optimum Data Base Reorganization Points." *Communications of the ACM* 16 (1973) 6: 362–65. Provides a formulation of the reorganization problem; however, its solution in an actual data base environment was not tested.

Siler, Kenneth F. "A Stochastic Evaluation Model for Data Base Organizations in Data Retrieval Systems." *Communications of the ACM* 19 (1976) 2: 84–95. Discusses a simulation model of a data retrieval system that significantly reduces the cost of experimenting in access path determination. Validation was subjective.

Smith, John Miles, and Chang, Philip Yen-Tang. "Optimizing the Performance of a Relational Algebra Interface." *Communications of the ACM* 18 (1975) 10: 568–79. Describes a "smart" interface to support a relational view of data using automatic programming. An actual implementation was not described.

Teichroew, D., and Hershey, E. A. "PSL/PSA: A Computer-Aided Technique for Structured Documentation and Analysis of Information Processing Systems." *IEEE Transactions on Software Engineering* SE-3 (1977) 1: 41-48. Reports on a technique and a commercially available package for documentation and systems analysis. PSL/PSA is one of the few feasible extensive-capability systems offered on the market and still under development.

Tuel, William G., Jr., "Optimum Reorganization Points for Linearly Growing Files." *ACM Transactions on Database Systems* 3 (March 1978) 1: 32-40. The problem of finding optimal reorganization intervals for linearly growing files is solved. Both the optimum and approximate policies are compared to previously published results using a numerical example.

van der Pool, J. A. "Optimum Storage Allocation for a File in Steady State." *IBM Journal of Research and Development* 17 (1973) 1: 27-38. Presents a formula-driven method of bucket size determination for files in steady state (additions to and deletions from file are equal). No report of an actual test case was made.

van der Pool, J. A. "Optimum Storage Allocation for a File with Open Addressing." *IBM Journal of Research and Development* 17 (1973) 2: 106-14. Finds minimum retrieval costs as a function of storage space and access characteristics but does not report on a practical implementation of the model.

van der Pool, J. A. "Optimum Storage Allocation for Initial Loading of a File." *IBM Journal of Research and Development* 16 (1972) 6: 579-86. Provides a simple formula-driven method of bucket size determination assuming hashing is used during initial file load operations. A practical implementation, if done, was not reported.

Wang, C. P., and Wedekind, H. H. "Segment Synthesis in Logical Data Base Design." *IBM Journal of Research and Development* (January 1975): 71-77. Presents an approach to logical data base design that employs the functional relation to represent relevant concepts in an application by removing redundant relations and relation reduction. Thus, a set of optimal relations is derived. An artificial example was discussed.

Yao, S. B.; Das, K. S.; and Teorey, T. J. "A Dynamic Database Reorganization Algorithm." *ACM Transactions on Database Systems* 1 (June 1976) 2: 159-74. Provides a reorganization algorithm for cases involving unknown data base lifetime and nonlinear performance deterioration.

APPENDIX C

CHAPTER QUESTIONS

CHAPTER 1

1. Explain the concept of data base system. In particular, differentiate it from conventional, dedicated file systems.
2. Attempt to classify the typical changes to applications and data that a DBMS might facilitate.
3. Enumerate the major operational entities of the CODASYL model of DBMS operation. In addition, trace the flow that occurs during a call for data retrieval.
4. Based on the CODASYL model of DBMS operation, what do you suppose will be its advantages and disadvantages?

CHAPTER 2

1. Many advantages and disadvantages of commercial DBMSs have been suggested. Attempt to map one into the other; that is, trace each claimed advantage into its cost, or disadvantage.
2. Cite a number of operational environments and identify the most important features of DBMSs in each case. Most important, are there any operational environments where DBMS disadvantages outweigh the advantages?
3. Are any there methods for minimizing DBMS installation costs or continuing costs?
4. As a DBA, how would you select the appropriate situations to introduce redundancy into physical storage?

CHAPTER 3

1. Why are data structure (logical) and storage structure (physical) used to partition data base terminology?
2. Distinguish between the concepts of extract and request.
3. Describe the data base design activities of clustering and partitioning. In particular, is one more useful than the other under certain conditions?

CHAPTER 4

1. Cite a number of possible application environments and discuss the issue of selecting a standardized or specialized DBMS.
2. Under what conditions should either procedural or nonprocedural languages (DMLs) be used?
3. Assuming that the network data model is the most general (of list, tree, and network models) why not always select it? When should the relational model be considered?
4. What problems might be anticipated when using the relational approach?
5. What must be done to convert a network structure to a tree; a tree to a list?

CHAPTER 5

1. Attempt to explode each of the data base design tasks into a number of specific elements.
2. A taxonomy of the data base design activity was presented; what other ways are there to partition the activities composing the taxonomy and how might they be used?
3. If faced with a number of DBDAs for a particular problem, what design-aid characteristics might assist you in the selection decision?

CHAPTER 6

1. User requirements definition is, at best, a difficult process. What general methodologies can be applied to it? Is there an effective way to avoid the problem, rather than to solve it?
2. Explain the theory behind the author's method of defining a clean set of attribute requirements. Under what conditions, if any, does it become impractical?
3. Discuss the strengths and weaknesses of IBM's Time Automated Grid technique, based on the introduction provided in this chapter.
4. Accurately Defined Systems, by NCR, employs a series of five forms to collect, define, and filter user requirements. Explain each and their relationship.
5. Of TAG and ADS, which is the most effective as a requirements definition methodology? Justify your answer.

CHAPTER 7

1. Logical Support Description has a number of applicable methodologies. Under what operational conditions would you select one method over another? That is, can you define a prescriptive rule for applying these techniques?

2. Explain in a short paragraph or statement the operation of the DBDA by Patt. Identify, in addition, any implicit assumptions made in the model.

3. What are the practical implications of applying IBM's Data Base Design Aid? For example, considering the potential benefits, is it likely to be a time-consuming activity?

4. What general statements can be made based on the contents of Figures 7.2-7.4 by Blasgen and Eswaran?

CHAPTER 8

1. A wide variety of physical support definiton methodologies are available. Why have so few of them become accepted in practice?

2. Why do you suppose that the current DBMS offerings do not include a prescriptive utility to assist the DBA in physical design and redesign?

3. Many of the design aids presented in this chapter rely on some expression of file or attribute access activity. What cost-effective methods exist for collecting this statistic?

4. The cost of computing is dropping each year. Physical design for efficiency is therefore becoming unimportant. Please comment.

5. What is the value of using a heuristic solution, rather than, for example, a mathematic programming or closed-form solution, to any given physical design problem?

6. Are there any secondary storage technologies for which record ordering or indexing is unimportant or unnecessary?

CHAPTER 9

1. Identify the major conceptual differences between an application-specific system and one supported by a DBMS from a user's point of view.

2. Do you believe that the user/provider problem is characteristic of data base environments, or simply aggravated by them?

3. Resolution of conflicting user demands may, at times, be very difficult. Would a corporate information policy committee alleviate this problem? If so, how would you staff it (what areas would be represented and from what level would the managers come)?

4. Should the individual who represents the DBA activity and who acts as liason with user departments have a different set of background and capability than that required for purely technical problems?

5. Do you foresee the nature of the user-DBA relationship changing over time? If so, for what reasons?

CHAPTER 10

1. Typically, programmers are required to make many decisions affecting system performance, in which the user has a vested interest. What are some of these performance parameters (requirements) and how might they be collected prior to system implementation?
2. The range of programmed solutions to a given user request is limited by hardware/software constraints. Who should decide, given a range of solutions, which should be selected?
3. What organizational problems would you forecast as resulting from the DBA imposing constraints on application programmers to which they do not directly report?
4. Why is system validation (for check points, etc.) and test so crucial in a DBMS environment?
5. Does the use of advanced programming methodologies affect the DBA's activity? If so, how?

CAPTER 11

1. Many commercial DD/Ds only support data descriptions. What additional useful capabilities are offered by allowing process description? Might these capabilities be used frequently enough to warrant the additional effort?
2. Outline the potential advantages of an active DD/D. What additional costs are there? Is it practical to begin DBMS operation with a passive DD/D and convert to an active use at a later time?
3. What problems do you foresee in defining and initializing the DD/D? Are the problems primarily technical, logical, political, or other?
4. The DD/D contains a wide variety of information. How might it be secured to avoid potential intentional and unintentional threats? May any of your recommendations be programmed?

CHAPTER 12

1. According to data presented in Chapter 12, DBAs believe that their role is primarily technical. Is this likely to change? Why?
2. Under what conditions would you advocate either the functional or application specialization of the DBA activity? Justify your answer. Also, are there any special cases requiring a different organizational structure? If so describe in detail.

CHAPTER 13

1. Under what conditions might one want to select a hardware monitor over one implemented in software?
2. How can sampling techniques be applied to reduce system overhead?
3. State a number of data base performance problem scenarios, then select a set of parameters that would permit the localization of the cause. Are there multiple measures that may be applied to confirm your analysis?
4. Are there any conditions under which performance monitoring is unnecessary? If so, what are they? Justify your position.

CHAPTER 14

1. What characteristics of advanced data processing systems make them difficult to audit?
2. Given that there exists an accepted standard approach to DBMSs (CODASYL's DBTG), what are the pros and cons of a standard interface between DBMS and audit software?
3. Define several operational environments, then select a set of audit techniques for application. Justify your choice.
4. Certified software (that is, software that has been reviewed in detail and has been "certified" as possessing certain properties) may be an alternative to the auditor understanding a complete system. Comment.
5. Pattern recognition techniques might well be applied to auditing, in general, and detection of fraud, in particular. Comment.

CHAPTER 15

1. For the purposes of this book, performance improvement is taken to mean performance tuning for efficiency. Why must the DBA become involved in an area that is primarily of a systems programming nature?
2. Systems simulators appear to offer many advantages over analytic techniques for complex problems. Cite a number of efficiency problems and determine whether analytic methods can be applied reasonably.
3. Under what conditions might data compaction be desirable? What methods may be used?
4. Choose any arbitrary compaction technique and estimate the operational overhead resulting from its use. Would this overhead be tolerable in many cases?

CHAPTER 16

1. Cite a number of operational environments, then determine the relevance

of the suggested advantages and disadvantages. What is your conclusion regarding the applicability of DBMS technology in these environments?

2. If one were to develop an equation of utility from the factors discussed, how might the coefficients (weights) be determined?

3. Discuss the rank ordering of the advantages and disadvantages contained in Tables 16.1 and 16.2. In particular, were you surprised at the results?

4. According to the study by Wiorkowski and Wiorkowski, operational costs increased by 25 percent relative to the nondata base systems. Do you feel this is an unreasonable premium in many cases? Be specific and justify your answer.

CHAPTER 17

1. Ideally, one should prepare for DBMS installation far in advance. If this is not possible, what tasks might be overlapped with little detrimental effect?

2. User knowledge of the data base concept has been stressed. In particular, with which concepts must users be familiar; with which need they not be concerned?

3. At the time of conversion one has the choice of implementing existing systems or rethinking the procedures and exploiting DBMS technology in their support. Identify the tradeoffs involved in the decision.

4. Argue the issue of DBA versus application programmer definition of subschemas.

5. Are there any apparent implementation advantages of standardized versus specialized DBMSs? If so, what are they?

CHAPTER 18

1. In a sense, a data base machine is an extended-capability data base I/O controller. As such, what potential does it have both in off-loading work from the main computer as well as performing functions not supported by conventional architectures?

2. Associative processing is likely to have a tremendous effect on data base applications. Consider the problem of physical data base design. What effect is it likely to have in this area?

3. Identify and discuss, in general, the effects of associative processing on all types of data base languages, including data definition, data manipulation, and query.

4. Nonprocedural query facilities are offered by many DBMS vendors. Comment on the specialized needs of users that may be serviced only through such a facility.

APPENDIX D

GLOSSARY

LOGICAL TERMS

access method

The means by which physical records are retrieved; typically indicating whether indexes, hashing, etc. are used.

access path

The sequential transformations necessary for a system to locate the physical record for a query.

activity ratio

The proportion of records that have to be inspected and/or updated during a given processing run in relation to the total number of records in the file.

add-delete request (ADR)

A request, made to the data base, that results in either a new record being added or an existing record being deleted.

attribute

A characteristic or descriptor of an entity. Each relevant attribute of an entity has a value associated with it indicating the extent to which that attribute is achieved.

attribute access probability

The relative likelihood that any given attribute, out of all occurrences of that attribute, will be inspected and/or updated during a given processing run.

attribute-name

A logical identifier of an attribute.

attribute-value

Each relevant attribute of an entity must have an associated value that indicates the extent to which that property has been achieved; for example, the value "brown" might be associated with the attribute "color".

candidate key

An identifier that uniquely determines which record is to be accessed.

chain

One of several possible logical organizations of records that has one entry point and one exit point, and to reach any desired record one must sequentially scan the chain; a special case of a chain is a ring structure whose last pointer to the next record points back to the first or entry point record.

currency

An attribute of data describing how recently the data for which a value exists was collected.

data aggregate

A named grouping of attributes, or data items.

data item

The smallest amount of named data; an attribute.

data structure

The logical organization of attributes or data items within the data base; this should be contrasted with storage structure, the physical arrangement of data in storage.

DDL (data definition language)

A language that has been standardized by CODASYL for describing schemas and subschemas. The subschema is described in the subschema DDL; the schema is the schema DDL. Since these are used to provide a degree of data independence where one is mapped into the other, they are in fact different.

degree	The number of domains in a relation.
domains	An attribute of a relation represented by a column in a table.
DMCL (device/media control language)	A language used to describe physical characteristics of the storage and access systems in a computer and controls storage assignments and interaction with the schema. The DMCL has not been standardized, since it is computer system dependent.
DML (data manipulation language)	A language standardized by CODASYL for procedurally defining access patterns and retrieval techniques for users of the data base. Currently CODASYL has defined standards for COBOL and FORTRAN when each is used as a host language but is enriched to include a number of high-level verbs for retrieval operations.
entity	The subject of inquiry, described in terms of attributes.
extract	A desired retrieval operation to the data base, consisting of one or more attributes on which to base the selection from among all records and the data to be returned.
hit ratio	The ratio of the number of accessed records to the total number of records of the same type(s).
inverted file	Any file whose contents can be accessed by defining a specific attribute value. This is accomplished through the use of an inverted list that indexes every record containing a specific value for a given attribute.

logical data base	The user's conception of the data base contents and organization. In addition there may exist a global logical data base organization conceived by the data base administration.
logical file	The logical organization of records as conceived by a user.
logical record	A user's conception of a set of related attributes describing an entity.
logical record occurrence	A data base may contain a number of logical records of each type for a user; each record is a logical record occurrence.
logical twin	Frequently, descriptions of entities associated with some other entity are put into a chain, each member of which is a logical twin of the other members. The offspring of a parent might be conceived of as a chain of variable length, with each occurrence of a record representing a child.
member record	A single record occurrence out of a set or file of records.
m-to-n relationship	A general measure of relationship complexity involving m association in one direction and n in the other.
network	Any logical structure allowing more than one entry point to any node and multiple exit points.
order criterion	The attribute that serves as a key for ordering data.
owner record	The record from which access was gained to some lower level or detail record.

primary key	An attribute that uniquely identifies a logical record.
schema	The global description of a data base; not just that for a particular application.
secondary key	An attribute serving to select one or a set of records from a data base but not guaranteeing uniqueness.
selection criterion	The set of one or more attributes used to define those records to be retrieved from the data base.
set	A term used by CODASYL's conceptualization of data base systems to describe a number of record occurrences with some general property.
logical data base	That data base described by the schema which is the union of all user data bases.
projection schema	Those attributes composing the set required for retrieval by the user.
read-only request	A retrieval from the data base consisting only of the read operation.
relation	A two-dimensional array of data elements describing some fact or set of facts.
request	A general, but complex, type of operation on a data base, recognizing that the retrieval may be expressed in terms of compound conditions.
tree	A common data structure in which each node has at most one entry point and any number of exit points.
tuples	A group of related elements.

value modification request	A request involving rewriting a previously stored value.
virtual data	Data that must be derived based on other stored data items.

PHYSICAL TERMS

access time	The summation of all the delays inherent in the process of retrieving data, usually consisting of seek time, rotational, and switching delays.
address	A unique identifier for the physical position within a datum or instruction in storage.
area	A subset of secondary storage where physical records are stored. A given area is characterized by capacity, access time, etc.
back end	A specialized processor that receives instructions and data from a main, general purpose processor, and stores, retrieves, and processes data from a physical file system connected to it; the back end is under the control of the main processor.
binding	The process of mapping logical or symbolic references to data to physical addresses and vice versa. This process may be done at coding time or during execution.
block	A set of data treated as a unit by the computer for purposes of transfer. Typically, the smallest amount of physically movable data is a physical record.
blocking factor	The number of logical records comprising a physical record or block. Records are blocked for purposes of efficiency.

buffer	A staging location within memory, used to temporarily hold physical records or block between I/O operations. Allowing multiple buffers for physical records in many cases reduces effective access time.
cell	A set of contiguous storage locations that are treated as a group in retrieval operations. If retrieval involves crossing a cell boundary an incremental delay is usually incurred.
clustering	The process of mapping the logical data base into physical records and may result in a given attribute or item being put in more than one physical record, thus creating redundancy. Without redundancy this is called partitioning.
cylinder	A set of one or more tracks lying in the same radial position of a disk pack and within which retrieval can be made without incurring a seek delay.
data set	A named collection of physical records that contain logically related data items in a prescribed arrangement; a physical file.
extent	A group of contiguous physical records contained in secondary storage.
field	The smallest unit of named data in a physical record.
front-end	A specialized processor typically used to handle I/O from external sources or other computer systems in a network.

partitioning	As with clustering, the process of mapping the logical data base into physical records but without redundancy.
physical data base	The physical representation of the logical data base that resides on secondary storage.
physical file	The physical grouping of one or more related physical records in secondary storage.
physical index	A physical collection of entries, often in tabular form, used to identify locations or associations of named items.
physical record	A set of data treated as a unit by the computer for purposes of transfer; a block.
primary storage	The main memory within the central processing unit, containing data and instructions.
redundancy	The repetition of components, information, data, etc. for purposes of security or retrieval efficiency.
rotational delay	The access time delay component involving physical passage (rotation) of the storage medium under the read/write head until the desired block is reached. This is also referred to as latency, and is usually smaller in magnitude than seek time but larger than switching delay.
secondary storage	The portion of memory in a computer system accessible through a channel, usually composed of tape, disk, etc.
seek delay	Usually, the largest magnitude delay component of access time, incurred

because of the physical positioning of the read/write heads to the appropriate track or cylinder.

storage structure — The physical relationships existing in secondary storage, such as the physical location of records in an area.

subfile — A collection of physically disjoint physical records.

subrecord — A subset of a physical record in secondary storage.

subschema — The description of the data items or aggregates relating to a specific program's view of the data base.

switching delay — Usually, the smallest delay component of access time to secondary storage, involving the electronic connection of specific read/write heads to the data transfer channel.

track — The series of physically adjacent storage locations whose contents are retrievable without changing read/write head positioning.

APPENDIX E

COMMONLY USED ACRONYMS

ACM	Association for Computing Machinery
ADR	Addition/Deletion Request
ADS	Accurately Defined Systems
BEA	Bond Energy Algorithm
CASE	Computer-Aided Input Evaluation
CODASYL	The Conference on Data Systems Languages
DBA	Data Base Administrator
DBDA	Data Base Design Aid
DBMS	Data Base Management System
DBTG	Data Base Task Group
DD/D	Data Dictionary/Directory
DDL	Data Definition Language
DL/I	Data Language I
DMCL	Device/Media Control Language
DML	Data Manipulation Language
DP	Data Processing
FOREM	File Organization Evaluation Model
I/O	Input/Output
IPS	Information Processing System
ISDOS	Information Systems Design and Optimization System
JCL	Job Control Language
LSD	Logical Support Description
LSI	Large Scale Integrated Circuit
OC	Order Criterion
PS	Projection Schema
PSA	Problem Statement Analyzer

PSD	Physical Support Definition
PSL	Problem Statement Language
ROR	Read Only Request
SC	Selection Criterion
SCS	Selection Criterion Set
SCERT	Systems and Computers Evaluation and Review Technique
TAG	Time Automated Grid Technique
URD	User Requirements Definition
VMR	Value Modification Request

INDEX

access method, 26
access path, 28, 103, 107
access time, 28
accessibility, 17
activity ratio, 28
addition/deletion request (ADR), 26, 28
address, 31
ADS (Accurately Defined Systems), 62, 68, 74, 82
algebra, 37, 38
area, 31
associative processor, 188, 190
Astrahan, M. M., et al., 80, 82
attribute, 23–24
attribute access probability, 28
audit, 159–67
audit techniques, 161–66

Babad, J. M., 101
Benner, F. H., 101
binding, 20, 31
Blasgen, M. W., et al., 80, 82, 83, 88–92
block, 31
blocking factor, 31
Bloom, B. H., 101

calculus, 37, 38
candidate key, 24
Cardenas, A. F., 101
CASE (Computer-Audited System Evaluation), 172, 174–75
Casey, R. G., 80, 82

cell, 31
centralized control of data, 14
chain, 24, 26
Chandy, K. M., et al., 101
clustering, 29, 31, 103
CODASYL, 7–10
Codd, E. F., 14
Coffman, E. G., et al., 80, 82
Collmeyer, A. J., et al., 101
commercial DBMSs, 44, 48
complexity, 12, 14, 20, 21
content analysis, 64–75
costs, 18–20, 34–35
currency, 24, 60
cylinder, 28–29

data aggregate, 24
data base: advantages, 11–18, 179–83; definition, 3; disadvantages, 18–22, 179–83; operation, 3–9
data base administrator (DBA), 112–21, 122–29, 131–39, 140–47
data base design aid (DBDA), 54–57, 85–86
data base machine, 187–88, 190
data compaction, 173
data definition language (DDL), 7–9, 38–44, 126–28
data dictionary/directory (DD/D), 129, 131–39, 143, 185, 186
data manipulation language (DML), 7–9, 33, 36–38
data set, 29
DBTG (data base task group), 7–9, 34
Dearnly, P., 79, 80, 101

231

ABOUT THE AUTHOR

JON D. CLARK received his BA in Industrial Administration at Michigan State University in 1968, his MBA at Eastern Michigan University in 1972, and the Ph.D. in Management at Case Western Reserve University in 1976. He has published many articles on data base and computer performance evaluation and a monograph on physical record design. Dr. Clark was Assistant Professor of Information Systems at the University of Texas at Dallas from 1975 to 1979 and is now Associate Professor of Accounting and Information Systems at North Texas State University.